what's so funny
aBOuT FAItH?

what's so funny
aBOuT FAItH?

JAKE MARTIN, SJ

a MeMOIR FRoM THE iNTERSeCTION
oF HILaRIOuS AND HOLy

LOYOLA PRESS.
A JESUIT MINISTRY
Chicago

LOYOLAPRESS.
A JESUIT MINISTRY

3441 N. Ashland Avenue
Chicago, Illinois 60657
(800) 621-1008
www.loyolapress.com

Art credit: © istockphoto.com and Jill Arena

Library of Congress Cataloging-in-Publication Data
Martin, Jake.
  What's so funny about faith? : a memoir from the intersection of hilarious and holy / Jake
Martin.
      p. cm.
  ISBN-13: 978-0-8294-3739-3
  ISBN-10: 0-8294-3739-8
1. Martin, Jake. 2. Jesuits--United States.--Biography. I. Title.
  BX4705.M3677A3 2012
  271'.5302—dc23
[B]

2012019998

Printed in the United States of America.
12 13 14 15 16 17 Bang 10 9 8 7 6 5 4 3 2 1

Contents

Live from New York, It's . . . a Jesuit?

Are you still sick?" It was my mother, of course.

"Yes, very," I mumbled through a tunnel of sleep and sinusitis. It was Sunday night and I was trying to get enough rest and fluids so I wouldn't have to call in sick the next morning. It's rather embarrassing to call in sick as a teacher when you live at the high school.

Yes, I live at my job. That is one of the blessings and curses of being a vowed religious: you live where you work. This can be a good thing, especially when you live in Chicago in mid-January and do not like getting up early. The bad part of it is, well, you live where you work—and among other things that can make the Sunday-night back-to-work blues that much grimmer.

So when my mother called to check up on me that Sunday night, I was not in the best of moods. I had missed our regular Sunday Mass and breakfast with her, my stepfather, and my grandmother because of my illness, and she was using her concern about my sinus condition as a decoy for what was really on her mind.

"When do you leave for New York?" she asked with feigned innocence, but she was already showing her hand.

"Thursday night. I hope my head is cleared up; I don't want to fly with a sinus infection."

"If you can, you should try to stop by," she said (*Here we go*, I thought) "Tomorrow or Tuesday. I work on Wednesday night, but I'd like to see you before . . ."

She stopped. She had gone too far and she knew it. There was a long pause before I finished the sentence:

"Before the plane crashes?"

She started laughing, "You know me too well!"

My mother, you see, is an amazing woman: smart, funny, and remarkable at most everything she does. Her sole flaw it seems, outside of a propensity for singing loudly and off key, is having the terribly Irish trait of assuming the worst outcome for every situation. I am no psychologist, but I would suspect it works as some sort of protective measure. If you assume that the worst will happen, either it will not happen or you will at least be prepared for it when it does.

Hence my impending plane crash in three days' time—my mother gets to work early on her worries. We finished our conversation as we always did, with much laughter, as I continued to rib her about her remarkable psychic abilities and to offer faint promises of stopping by before I left for New York.

As it happens, I did not visit and my plane did not crash—although it was delayed, and I wound up landing at JFK at around ten-thirty on Thursday night, an hour and a half after my expected arrival time. I was staying at the Jesuit residence on Fourteenth Street in Manhattan, a good forty-five-minute trip from JFK, and I had told Don Gannon, the rector, to expect me around ten o'clock. I didn't have Don or any other community member's phone number and had no way to get in contact with anyone, especially so late in the evening. I was not prepared—which was not unusual.

As a small boy growing up with multiple interests, most of which related to watching television and none of which related to school work, I had learned very early how to get things done with little or no preparation. I liked to call this skill living in the moment, while my parents and teachers liked to call it just plain lazy. In any event, my ability to wing it had only been enhanced during my years of working in improvisational comedy. I had learned how to perform without using a script and how to go onstage and make things up as I went along. I transferred this skill to my stand-up comedy as well. In the world of stand-up comedy, most comics performed with a full set of prepared jokes. I preferred to improvise, as I found that something was lost in the intensity and immediacy of the delivery when I was reciting something I'd memorized beforehand.

This skill had served me well, even as I transitioned into the seemingly hyperstructured world of religious life. I took Jesus at his word when he said, "Therefore I tell you, do not worry about your life" (Matthew 6:25–34)—although I'm sure many of my superiors would have preferred that I hadn't taken Jesus so literally and had been a bit more prepared for some things, like teaching, for instance.

Now I was going to be really late, and I had no way of letting anyone know. I was afraid that nobody would hear the doorbell from upstairs, where the Jesuits slept at the Four-teenth Street residence, and that I would be stuck sleeping in the doorway—or worse, that I would have to take the subway across town to sleep on the sofa at my sister's cramped apart-ment that she shared with a roommate.

I walked out to the transportation area of JFK, dragging along my red *America* magazine duffel bag stretched to the seams with books and clothing so as to avoid the extra cost of checked luggage, and looked for a cab. A man immediately approached me and asked if I wanted to take a limo for the same cost as a cab. My parents had introduced me to the world of rogue limo drivers at New York airports, so, though a bit unsettled by having to make a fifteen-minute walk across JFK to a parking lot located somewhere near the Long Island bor-der, I accepted.

Sitting in the backseat of the limo, taking in the less-than-stellar sights of residential Queens and too awake from the cof-fee I'd had at the airport, I began to reflect on my day. This was nothing unusual or out of the ordinary. As a matter of fact, I and thousands of other Jesuits do this very thing every day (sometimes twice a day) as part of our normal routine. Jesuits do not have the same type of regimented schedules of other religious congregations such as the Trappists or the Bene-dictines, but we do have some set practices we're expected to complete on a daily basis. The Examen is the most impor-tant of these practices, according to our founder, St. Ignatius of Loyola.

The Examen is at the heart of our charism, or spiritual purpose. It's the ability to reflect on our work, our relation-ships with others, and where we find God throughout the day.

It's also our primary tool for discernment; it helps us identify where God is calling us to be and what actions to take.

As I looked around at the interior of the limo—stained carpeting and chipped glasses laid out on the dusty wet bar, the picture of ersatz opulence—the absurdity of the situation struck me, and I smiled. Who says God does not have a sense of humor?

Since the age of four, when I would sneak downstairs, way past my bedtime, to the family den hoping to catch a glimpse of NBC's cutting-edge sketch-comedy show *Saturday Night Live*, I had dreamed of going to New York and becoming a comedian. This was followed by years of classes, shows, and auditions; of waiting tables and answering phones to pay the rent; of going to sleep hungry and watching my friends pass me by while I bided my time in Chicago, hoping to catch that one break that would finally bring me to New York, with all its attached fame and glory.

Well, here I was, in New York, all set to perform on Saturday night. The punch line was that this was not quite how I'd envisioned it as a four-year-old—or even as a twenty-four-year-old. In my dreams there was a limo, of course, but I didn't have to walk halfway across JFK carrying my own bag to get there. Then there was that whole Jesuit thing: for the past seven years I had been a member of the Society of Jesus; I had taken vows of poverty, chastity, and obedience. I lived in community, owned no property, did not date, and had to ask my superior for permission to come here. And finally there was the venue: the Creek in Long Island City was not exactly 30 Rockefeller Center, the home of *Saturday Night Live*.

It was midnight when I arrived at the Fourteenth Street residence. After a few fruitless knocks, Don finally heard me from his room two floors above; mercifully, I didn't have to sleep in the doorway. In my room, I began to unpack when I remembered one of the most important matters. Not wanting to deal with the repercussions of forgetting, I grabbed my phone. It was late, but I knew it wouldn't matter. "I'm here and the plane didn't crash!" Mom laughed.

My sister Amanda lives on the Upper East Side, but not *that* Upper East Side. She shares less than four hundred square feet and two bedrooms with a roommate on First Avenue, about as far away as you can get from the old money and fast-living types closer to Central Park. She works as a math teacher in the South Bronx and has been doing so since she finished school five years ago. She is the size and stature of a porcelain doll, but she is made of steel, far tougher than her big brother. My sister is my hero and is definitely the macho one in the family.

My sister and her boyfriend, Jay, were enraptured as they stood in front of the Twin Donut on Fourteenth and Sixth, staring into his palm, oblivious to the chaos of New York on a Saturday night. As I approached, I attempted to make eye contact to no avail. It wasn't until I stood in front of them that they acknowledged me.

"What is it?" I asked.

"It's amazing!" my sister replied, "You have to see this!"

I heard the strains of a high-pitched voice coming from Jay's palm. "Here, look," Jay said, and showed me the tiny electronic device that seemed to hold all the secrets of the world. He had pulled up a clip from YouTube, and I watched as a baby monkey rode backward on a pig around a fenced-in area while a man sang in falsetto a word-for-word account of the event. With more than two million hits at that time, this was quite the big deal.

"Cute," I sniffed halfheartedly, but an hour before show time was ironically the least likely time for me to find something funny, baby monkey or no baby monkey. In my head I questioned the wisdom of asking my sister and Jay to accompany me to the show, and I thought it would have been better to just make the trek to Queens on my own.

It wasn't that I didn't want to be around them; I am just not particularly available mentally right before I go on stage. Part of it is nerves, but another part is just going through variations of things that I would like to talk about during my set.

I had spent the afternoon in my room at Fourteenth Street performing to an audience of none. Facing the wall, coffee in hand, I went through several variations of eight-minute sets of jokes (the time allotted me that evening), none of which I would use or had any intention of using. As I said, I usually improvise my stand-up—but I like to prepare anyway, as it gives me some sense of control. The idea of going onstage with nothing prepared terrifies me, even though I know that I will wind up not using anything I've concocted but will go with whatever strikes me as funny five minutes before I head onstage.

We got off the 7 train and looked around for the venue. This was bare-bones show biz; there were no marquees in this neighborhood, no flashing lights, and no handlers to be had. It was just me walking through Queens looking for a sign. I found the place and peeked into the window. The stage was big, much bigger than I expected, and there appeared to be a good number of seats. I was not supposed to check in for another half hour and didn't want to hang out at the venue, so we went to the bodega across the street, where I grabbed a gigantic bottle of water to use for hydration purposes as well as a prop.

After watching the baby monkey riding backward on a pig yet again and finding it no funnier on the dark empty street, I decided to stop putting off the inevitable and headed to the venue. I was directed to a stairwell, and it was then that I realized that I would not be performing on the big stage I had spied through the window but instead would be heading to the stage downstairs.

At the bottom of the stairs was a bar. Now, this venue I knew. There were a handful of tables in front of a small raised area with a microphone and some speakers; this was my stage. I turned to my sister and said, "I have no idea why I put myself through this." But I did—I knew very well.

Eight years before, I'd sat in a similar bar in Chicago. I had just completed a show and was engaging in the traditional postmortem with my fellow comics. As was usually the case in these scenarios, after the initial back-and-forth banter among all parties, the conversation splintered among individuals, and I began talking with my friend Elaine. Elaine had been performing for years, had done shows everywhere, and at the time was becoming weary of the show-business grind. She had begun to find fulfillment in her day job and was slowly easing herself out of the world of comedy.

I spoke with her about a recent round of discouraging auditions and asked her why she hadn't gone out for any of them. "You know, I just don't love it," she said. "I did it because I was good at it and people laughed and I got a lot of attention and it seemed like a way to get famous. But I don't love it. I love singing, but I don't love comedy."

"Really?" I responded. "You don't?" It touched a nerve. Over the previous year I'd begun to question my own motives and whether or not comedy was enough to make me happy, because it had not been doing so lately. I had wanted to be on *Saturday Night Live* for as long as I could remember, and that obsession, that goal, had been enough to sustain me for a long time. But as I began to encounter people who did work on *Saturday Night Live*, I began to recognize that it was a job like any other job, and that if or when I attained that goal, it would not be enough to make me happy. I would be looking for the next thing, the next job that promised fulfillment.

This was not the only thing weighing on my mind that evening. My grandmother had recently passed away, and I'd begun to question my motives of another sort. I had not set foot in a church in nearly a decade, other than the obligatory Christmas appearance when visiting my parents. But I prayed. Every night before I went to bed I would say an Our Father and a Hail Mary. I prayed before takeoff on an airplane. I prayed before every show I did. Like many of my peers in comedy, I professed not to believe, yet my actions told a different story.

For a long time I had refused to admit even to myself that I believed. I told myself that my prayers were leftover childhood superstitions that did not mean anything. I enjoyed ridiculing people of faith, knocking down believers and those who professed faith. I reveled in pointing out their hypocrisy, yet it was becoming more and more difficult to ignore my own hypocrisy. Eight years later, in yet another anonymous bar on yet another anonymous Saturday night, I now knew why I still went up in front of a crowd of strangers and attempted to make them laugh.

"You're up fifth," the emcee told me. I nodded and got up and excused myself, leaving my sister and her boyfriend to their nachos and beer. I looked for a green room, the waiting area where performers could prepare backstage before a show, but there was none. This was the minor leagues of comedy; such trappings were for bigger, better stages. I headed to my only place of recourse.

A men's room in a bar might not be the most conducive spot for prayer, but it would have to do in a pinch, and this indeed was a pinch. The bathroom was about the size of a broom closet, but taking the tried-and-true Ignatian tenet of finding God in all things at face value, I got down on my knees on the dirty tile and began to chat with Christ.

I could boast of the fact that my spiritual life had progressed beyond the realm of "Dear God, please let me kill tonight!"—*kill* being the comic's term for having a great show. I was now a professional pray-er of a sort. I closed my eyes and tried to ignore the smell of excess bleach that permeated the cramped space; I saw myself in God's presence. My imagery in prayer tends to be similar to that of movies, so I pictured myself being shot by a camera from above as it zoomed up and out of the bathroom, out of the club, out of Queens, and on and on until I was but a mere speck in the universe, one teeny-tiny piece of the vast expanse of God's creation, but as necessary and as loved as I was infinitesimal.

On the cold, stained tile floor, I asked Christ to direct me and my thoughts and to help me accept whatever the outcome of the show might be. I then finished with the Anima Christi, a prayer commonly used by Jesuits and usually said at the end of each of the Spiritual Exercises of St. Ignatius. I crossed myself and flushed the toilet—because for some reason I felt self-conscious about praying in the bathroom—and walked out ready to perform.

The nachos were gone as I sat silently with my sister and her boyfriend, watching the other comics perform. The emcee came up behind me and asked, "Do you want me to say you're a priest?" "No." I was not about to get into it with him about the logistics of Jesuit formation at this juncture and why, though I was a member of the Society of Jesus for close to seven years, I would not in fact be a priest for another four. Still, he had brought up a rather urgent dilemma that I had yet to resolve. Did I let my audience know that I was a Jesuit, or did I not mention it?

I'd come up in a tradition of comedy that believed in unflinching truth: I believed that humor did not have to be manufactured or invented but rather came from our honest appraisals of our own lives and the lives of those around us. Being a Jesuit was such a huge component of who I was that it seemed uncomfortable to talk around it. Still, my announcement that I was studying to be a priest had met with some pretty lukewarm responses from audiences in the past. Heading to New York that weekend, I was resolute that I would not mention it, that I was a comic like everyone else, and that, just as many of them never mentioned their day jobs in their acts, neither did I have to mention mine, however enormous and consuming that "day job" might be.

People came to comedy clubs to be entertained, not to be freaked out by priests in training. What I found after seven years of day-to-day living to be a pretty normal mode of operation was foreign and frightening for others. I was a vowed religious, and for some the mere mention of the word *religion* put them on edge.

As the emcee called my name, I still had very little idea of what exactly I'd do. But I did say a little prayer as I walked toward the stage, a very little prayer. "Help me," said a very small voice deep from within. And as I began my set, it occurred to me that like everything else with comedy, it was not what you said but how you said it that made all the difference. It all depended on timing and delivery.

If I said my set was perfect, I'd be lying. It was too sloppy for me. I rushed through the last minute because I had such a good response to my talking about being a Jesuit—but comedy is not math and is not entirely reliant on precision. It is the most pragmatic of art forms, and at the end of the day the only thing that matters is if the audience laughed. I told the truth, the whole truth, and they laughed. They laughed!

The Real Housewives
of Cook County

Genes are important. For instance, I have good teeth. Not in color; they are perpetually off-white (or ecru, as I like to say, to make them sound classier) with a distinctive hint of tubercular yellow. But they're strong. I've never had a cavity in three and a half decades on this earth. Not one. I brag about this whenever I get the chance, which is surprisingly not that often. Usually, my only opportunities for dental grandstanding occur when an acquaintance or colleague is discussing his or her own upcoming sojourn to the dentist; that's when I make my move: "I've never had a cavity. Thirty-six years, not a one: nil, zip, zed. Teeth, 32; Cavities, 0." The response to this braggartism is a look that could be construed as either concern or awe. I prefer to believe the latter.

My people have strong teeth. I assume this is some evolutionary development related to having to tear through the flinty husk of one of the few remaining potatoes during the

Irish Famine. Whatever the reason, I'm sure it had something to do with food. My people love food, which is ironic considering that I come from a culture that, in its however many thousands of years of existence, has only managed to contribute corned beef, cabbage, and soda bread to the world's culinary landscape, and even those contributions are rather dubious. The corned-beef thing was probably stolen from the Jews, and soda bread . . . well, who wants to claim a food that has the consistency and texture of a mouthful of human hair?

Food is a family obsession. My mother in particular has spent the better part of her life in a love-hate relationship with it. What I'm trying to say, ever so gently, is that my mother was a fat kid (sorry, Mom!), and the impact of her fat childhood has rippled through my life with the same force that the water did when my mother's portly nine-year-old frame leapt into the deep end of the Fisk Park pool in Green Bay, Wisconsin.

According to legend, my mother was quite the swimmer. Quite the hefty swimmer, but a swimmer nonetheless, and I was expected to follow in her aquatic footsteps. By that I mean that I was supposed to learn how to swim for more than a minute and a half without having to touch my feet to the bottom of the pool. I never quite mastered this despite eleven years of swimming lessons. (No, I'm not lying: eleven years—stop judging me!)

Every summer since I was four my mother would cart me out to the local Y for another futile attempt at teaching me how to float, kick my feet, and move my arms at the same time. I would walk out onto the deck of the pool with all the other children, slowly climb into the water, and proceed to spend the next hour hanging from the side of the pool and talking to the other children while they took turns swimming back and forth across the pool.

"OK, Jake, now it's your turn," the instructor would say hopefully.

"No, that's OK. I'm all right here," I'd respond enthusiastically, hanging on to the side of the pool and turning back to my conversation about the three rules that would keep a Mogwai from turning into a gremlin—this was from the film of the same title that I was obsessed with throughout childhood.

The instructors learned pretty quickly not to force the issue. Swimming wasn't my thing, chatting was. Often I wound up chatting with the instructors themselves, usually about TV or movies, and they were always impressed with my encyclopedic knowledge of those subjects, in particular my ability to recite the entire contents of the *TV Guide* from memory. I'd avoid looking over at my mother, who I knew was gesturing to me from behind the Plexiglas window to stop talking and get swimming.

I had similar problems at school, duly noted on all my report cards: "Needs to practice self-control" was the one constant on all of them. It wasn't that I disliked school; on the contrary, I liked it very much—it was a wonderful social outlet. It was the schoolwork part I didn't particularly care for, as it interfered with my socializing and my doing impressions of my teachers and various other adults in my life. While I liked my third grade teacher Miss Hamilton just fine, I liked mimicking Miss Hamilton's yelling at me for talking even more—and more than that I loved the response it got from Sara Polaski who sat directly across from me and was my best and most loyal audience. Making people laugh was my favorite thing to do. It was a far more important part of my childhood reality than paying attention during Math or getting As. I preferred Bs and Cs because I didn't have to do much work to get them and so got to goof off as much as I liked. My mother was less than thrilled with this attitude. But I felt that it was at least partially her fault.

While it was never explicitly stated, it was communicated early on in my family that being able to make someone laugh was the greatest skill a person could possess. My mother came from a family of six children, five of whom were girls. I liked to call my mother and her sisters the Coven, primarily because, whenever two or more of them gathered, a bouquet of hyena-like cackles inevitably arose.

Perhaps this ability to laugh came from their Irish grandparents, who regaled them with stories of Pishlogue and Strielogue, a pair of numbskulls in the vein of Laurel and Hardy who floundered their way through the Mayo countryside of my great-grandmother's childhood. Perhaps it came from their being cursed with names that all sounded the same: Maureen, Kathleen, Eileen. Or perhaps they laughed a lot because they always took a backseat to their lone brother, my uncle Bill. Whatever the reason, my mother and her sisters were quick, sharp-witted women who didn't suffer fools gladly. Ask any of their first husbands.

When I refer to my family, I'm almost always referring to my mother and her sisters as well as their children. We were an incredibly tight-knit group. We spent almost every weekend together, usually at my grandparents' house near Chicago's Ravenswood Manor neighborhood.

Everything beautiful and joyful from my childhood is boxed up into that white stucco house on Sacramento Street, with its smell of baked chicken, Pall Mall cigarettes, and Emeraude perfume. My cousins and I were an assemblage of fresh-scraped knees, Kool-Aid mustaches, and palms gingerly cupping lightning bugs while Neil Diamond sang in the background and the Coven kicked up their heels and danced around the kitchen as dusk settled on a never-remembered date of an unforgettable late-summer night.

Amid all the cackles and euphoric gamboling it was easy for a kid to get lost. I learned early that if I was going to get any attention in the family—and I loved attention—I was going to have to earn it. So I decided I would be funny. This is sort of a chicken-or-egg thing, as I was my mother's firstborn and only child for the first nine years of my life, and as often happens with firstborn children, I was treated as the second coming of the Messiah. To this day my mother likes to brag that my very first word was *psychosomatic*, a bitter, bitter irony if ever there were one for this hypochondriac. What she fails to mention is that I was seven years old at the time of said utterance. Not really, but I was hardly the prodigy my mother claims me to be.

Everything I did was remarkable to my mother, to hear her tell it. I could have been comfortably seated at the Algonquin Round Table as a three-year-old. I was encouraged by her laughter, and my aunts were no better. I was the baby of the family for many years and was indulged and affirmed to the excess that often befalls those of that familial rank.

I wanted to be a part of the lightning-fast banter that went on between my mother and her sisters. I wanted to be able to make them laugh the way they made one another and the rest of the family laugh. I especially wanted to make my godmother laugh; to my mind, she was the funniest person in the world: Aunt Ginger.

My aunt Ginger was only thirteen years old when I was born, and I was told that, as my godmother, she was responsible for my spiritual well-being—she did this quite effectively, though perhaps not in the manner expected of her.

She still lived with my grandparents when I was a kid, and I was always impatient for the weekends when I could spend time with her there. I would go up to her room—with its hats hanging from the wall, the old movie posters, and the Irish flag, all of which I found to be too cool for school—and she would put on her favorite music, usually David Bowie or Elvis Costello, and would teach me how to dance punk rock, kicking my feet in front of me while thrashing my arms about.

We would go to such exotic locales as the Walgreens pharmacy or the neighborhood bodega to pick up a six-pack of Tab and cigarettes. Walking together, we would pretend to be French, speaking gibberish with a French accent or repeating the phrase "La plume de ma tante" over and over again, she smoking her usual Kool Mild 100 cigarette while I inhaled on a burnt-sienna Crayola.

We would make up songs, often parodies of popular music, such as by adapting the words to the then hugely popular Tears for Fears song "Shout" from the original: "Shout, shout, let it all out, these are things we can do without!" to "Shout, shout, let it all out, give me a hotdog with sour kraut!" Yes, brilliant! I'm amazed I wasn't signed to *Saturday Night Live* right then.

Speaking of which, I have my aunt to thank for introducing that particular obsession into my life. My earliest memory of watching the show was in 1979, when I was five years old. The show itself was only one year younger than I. I didn't understand the significance of it at the time, even while it was changing the face of comedy right before my eyes. I do remember hating the "Weekend Update" portion of the show because, as you can imagine, topical humor is never a favorite with kindergartners, and I found "Weekend Update" almost as interminably dull as the musical segments, which never featured Olivia Newton John or Big Bird, my two favorite musical acts at that time. I couldn't wait for the show to get back to the good stuff, like the Killer Bees and the Olympia Café sketch (of "Cheezboigah, cheezboigah" fame).

The only thing I did enjoy about the "Weekend Update" segment was Gilda Radner, and more specifically her character Roseanne Roseannadanna, the wild-haired, nasal-talking correspondent who always managed to digress from the subject at hand into a repulsive tangent about the unseemly bodily functions of various celebrities. Such as the time she gave an editorial about quitting smoking that quickly detoured into a soliloquy about the belly-button lint of Dr. Joyce Brothers.

Of course, her talk of nose hairs, boogers, and pimples was a veritable comedic horn of plenty to the ears of a five-year-old boy. That being said, there was something more to Gilda that transcended the gross-out humor of juvenile boys; there was a loving, humble compassion that informed all her characters and made her comedy something gentle and beautiful.

Gilda was perhaps the closest any performer has ever come yet to duplicating Charlie Chaplin. While Chaplin was primarily noted for one character, the Little Tramp, and Gilda for a collection of lovable misfits, what they both shared, unique to most performers but in particular to comedians, was a radiating vulnerability that struck an audience at a deeper level of which a joke or situation was ever capable.

The subversion of societal roles and expectations is a fundamental principle of comedy. The element of the sacred that can be found in comedy comes from the fleeting allocation of justice and rightness in an otherwise fundamentally unjust and broken world. What an audience finds humorous is the realization of a desire fulfilled, a subconscious truth that is being told, that is, the shift in power positions that are infrequently found in their daily lives. Often, what we think of as funny is simply the playing out of our own fantasies about justice—how we think things ought to be but never are; how we assume God would have things were it not for free will. We find the simplest examples of such wish fulfillment in such classic comedy scenarios as the snobby society doyenne getting a pie in the face; the billionaire being duped by the waif; or the poor student outsmarting his smug, wealthy classmate.

What comedy does—however fleeting and momentary it may prove—is empower the vulnerable and give a voice to the voiceless. Radner and Chaplin exemplify this truth, although nobody personified it better than the other comedic icon from my childhood: Richard Pryor.

Chaplin's Little Tramp is an icon for the ages; he personified the hopes and dreams of the downtrodden everywhere, and because all but one of his films was silent, that everywhere is unconstrained by the limitations of language. Chaplin's everywhere is global. While fundamentally a slapstick comedian, he was different from his peers, such as Harold Lloyd and Buster Keaton, primarily because of his gift for conveying a sincere depth of feeling through movement and facial expression. Still, slapstick or not, the humor came not so much from the pain he suffered through various pratfalls and missteps but rather through progression and discovery. The Little Tramp's misfortune came not from stupidity but from naïveté; he is an innocent and not a rube, which makes a significant difference in how an audience responds. Michael Scott, from the acclaimed American version of the television series *The Office*, never discovers or progresses; he is limited, and so an audience's response to him can only be one of contempt at worst, pity at best.

When we watch Michael Scott, we are readily aware that here is an incredibly witty and sharp actor portraying an incredibly stupid man. Steve Carell, the actor who portrays Michael Scott, never lets the audience forget for a minute that he is in on the joke. There is a certain hardness to Carell's portrayal, as the disdain he has for the character is palpable. While this isn't necessarily a bad thing comedically, it does put limits on the character and the ability of the comedy to move past the immediacy of the situation. What it becomes is nothing more than a white, middle-class male making fun of a white middle-class male. That's fine for what it is, but comedy has the potential to be much, much more than bourgeois, middlebrow status affirmation.

Chaplin knew this, Radner knew this, and no one knew it better than Pryor. Their comedy was not one of cerebral commentary or smugness, but of compassion, empathy, and growth. The characters they portrayed and the performances they gave were fully realized, fully exposed essays on the human condition—that is, our own sinfulness as well as our capacity for generosity and concern. Even a character as grotesque as Radner's Roseanne Roseannadanna was infused with love and consideration, most identifiable when the character transitioned into brief recollections of her father and referred to herself as "little Roseanne Roseannadanna." It is in those moments that we are able to catch a glimpse of the tenderness of human relationships that are necessary for our flourishing.

These moments, however brief, give us an intimacy with the character or performer that is important: they make us care for them, and the subsequent laughter they elicit comes from a place of commiseration and affection rather than judgment and disdain.

And if you thought I was already making comedy unfunny, here is the part where I make it *really* not funny.

Richard Pryor embodied comedy's ability to transcend, to move beyond the realm of the superficial into the realm of the cathartic and the political. In comedy, perhaps more so than any other art form, it is difficult to separate the artist from the work. The work of the comedian is not just the written, recited word—if there is even that—it is the physical body of the artist. The timing of the mind, the delivery of the voice and its inflection, the expressions of the face, the movement of the body—all these things are essential to the product, the work of the artist.

So much of what made Pryor's comedy remarkable was him: the enormous eyes; the gentle, pleading voice; the black halo of hair framing his head. His hunching of the neck and shoulders seemed to be the result of equal parts fear and fatigue. In spite of the ever-present mustache, so much of what made Pryor appealing was the childlike quality, the never-healed hurt that poured from those enormous, dark, saucer eyes. His body, this physical vessel through which the message came, was a huge part of how Pryor was able to soften his audience. First and foremost, your audience must be willing to listen to what you have to say.

But the physical Pryor was the result of the spiritual Pryor. Few, if any, comedians or performers have ever been as unflinchingly honest as he was. On a stage in front of twenty thousand people he bled his often-painful truth for all to see. Pryor didn't have time for jokes; he had far more interesting, more important things to do. Although his comedy was above all transcendent, it always began with him. He spoke in the first person, which not only is good etiquette in the therapeutic community but also is a helpful tool for the comedian who wants to voice critique on a larger scale but doesn't want to alienate his or her audience.

Pryor's own situation was that of a black man living in a white man's world, always "the other," regardless of his success or failure. His observations were most succinct and poignant when they were about people's reactions to him. Like all marginalized peoples, he did not enter a room alone; he entered a room burdened with a set of luggage he didn't pack.

His story, which he told for nearly three decades on empty stages across the world, was often the brutal truth-telling of the upper room, the prophesying of Galilee, and the final witness of Golgotha. Some people laughed, and that was enough, like the parabolic seeds drifting in the gale. But many in the audience heard more, and the laughter proved the only balm for a burning truth.

Pryor told his story: from being raised in a brothel by a prostitute mother and grandmother to his battle with addiction that culminated with him setting himself on fire. He exposed himself entirely, and while doing so, he exposed the world as well. He had a tacit agreement with his audience that if he was willing to disclose his own secrets and shortcomings, he expected them to do the same.

His comedy was not a full-on indictment of humanity, and that's important to note. Often comedians come from a place of total anger, which can focus and fuel their craft. But more often than not, their rage distorts and alienates, leaving an audience no other recourse than detachment.

At the least, Pryor made people laugh; at best, he changed the way people thought—not just about race, although to deny the import of what Pryor did and wanted to do in that area would be irresponsible. He had the ability to express the thoughts and feelings of the outsider and the alien in a way that they were incapable of articulating on their own.

Pryor and Chaplin offered insightful microcritiques of the contemporary social conditions in which they found themselves and a universal examination of the relationships between conventional society and the marginalized. What both did so successfully, and what makes their work so significant on a level outside the political, is their ability through the genre and their own talents to evoke compassion and understanding from an audience consisting primarily of members of mainstream culture. They helped raise the awareness of the condition of the outsider or the alien, and gently but firmly, they assigned culpability and insisted on accountability from their audience.

Gilda Radner's comedy, for various reasons, never reached the heights of Chaplin or Pryor; what she did do, however, on a less grand scale, was to claim a very public voice for the vulnerable. All her characters, from the aforementioned revolting Roseannadanna to the hearing-impaired Emily Litella and the fantasy-loving Girl Scout Judy Miller, were created with a loving, gentle concern. Radner demonstrated the beauty and power to be found in the oddball, the ugly duckling. Her portrayals insisted on the audience's regard and affection; she never ridiculed or pandered to her characters; rather, they became fully flourishing examples of a very different but valid human experience.

When I sat on the thick, green carpeting of my grandma's living room next to my aunt Ginger and watched Gilda Radner and Bill Murray essay the sweet yet ridiculous romance of "the Nerds," Lisa and Todd, I could not imagine that thirty years later I would still be laughing just as hard at that very same sketch—only this time on my laptop while watching it on YouTube.

And I couldn't have realized then, of course, that these silly people doing seemingly silly things in a television studio far, far away would have such a significant impact on my view of the world and my relationship with God. Through the qualities of transcendence, kindness, integrity, and compassion, these comedians articulated and embodied what would become foundation stones for my life as a Jesuit, for my life as someone whose mission is to help souls by finding God in all things.

Scooby Doo and the
Blessed Virgin, Too!

The radio alarm clock crowed loud and crackled. There was no music, just static and a man's voice talking about an unusually warm October in Chicago. I opened my eyes, slapped the alarm, and leaped as fast as I could over the freezing hardwood floor to the comfortable warmth of the carpeted hallway. It was Saturday morning, and there were cartoons to be watched.

I pulled my faded Incredible Hulk pajamas down over my six-year-old tummy and ran down the winding staircase of our old, drafty, Victorian fixer-upper.

I turned on our brand new Zenith and plopped down on the enormous blue sofa that I liked to make believe was the ocean, on which I floated safe and secure. I pretended to tread water on the plush fabric—as I'd seen my mother do in the pool at the Y—while I watched *Scooby-Doo, Where Are You!*, including special guest star Phyllis Diller, as they worked on getting to the bottom of the case of the lizard man and the haunted house.

I heard the rattling of the lock on the front door as I pushed my hands out beside me, trying to recall exactly how to tread. I was used to a steady flow of aunts, cousins, and grandparents clomping through the hallways, so I kept watching Scooby and pushing with my arms as I heard feet falling and words coming toward me.

Shaggy pulled the mask off the lizard man to reveal sweet old Mrs. Bigglesworth, as Scooby and the gang gasped. In my periphery I saw my mother floating, fast intruding on my sea. There was a pause. I kept my eyes on the television. "Jake, Daddy died this morning."

My father had been in the hospital since September. His timing was poor. I had just started the first grade and was learning how to put words in alphabetical order and write in cursive. He had Hodgkin's disease, something I knew little about other than that he occasionally had to go to the hospital and could not work full-time, so he stayed at home with me while my mom worked nights at an insurance agency. My dad helped me learn to read, tie my shoes, ride a bike, and practice writing my fives so they no longer looked like the letter S. Now entering the first grade, having to go to school all day for the first time, I needed him.

I was a worrier. They say genius is genetic; so is worry. My grandmother was quite skilled in the area, my mom perfected it, and I became the Picasso of worry. One night earlier that summer, Dad had stopped by my room to find me on my back on the hardwood floor.

"What are you doing? It's two in the morning!" He whispered, more confused than angry.

"I'm trying to make myself tired so I can fall asleep," I replied. "I'm really worried about taxes," I continued, while trying to keep my feet on the ground as I pulled my chin to my knees.

"Taxes were in April. You don't need to worry about Mom and me paying taxes."

"I'm not worrying about you. I'm worried about me," I said, rolling sideways on my back, trying to inch myself forward. "I don't know how to pay taxes."

"You don't pay taxes. You're six years old."

"But I will, and I don't know how to!" At that point, I expected my dad to pick me up and rub my face and take me downstairs to teach me the basics of the 1040 form. But he just started laughing, and although he did pick me up, he placed me in bed rather than in front of a calculator as I had hoped.

"You'll be fine," he said. I curled my toes and rubbed them into my mattress and quickly fell asleep. I was safe.

When my dad went to the hospital in September, I was sent to my aunt Carol's house in the suburbs. Aunt Carol was my dad's sister, and she lived in Highland Park, a suburb of Chicago, which might as well have been the darkest tropics of Africa for a kid who had never left the confines of the city. She and my Uncle Tom lived in a split-level house covered in wood paneling that seemed incredibly modern. They had a shower instead of a bathtub with feet; a dishwasher instead of just a sink; and there was no sign of the rattling, antiquated, cast-iron radiators that were in every room of our nearly hundred-year-old house.

More important, they had an enormous backyard with trees everywhere. One in particular had its branches placed just so, to make it perfect for climbing like they did on one of my favorite television shows, *Little House on the Prairie*.

In many ways, the week was idyllic. My arms ached from climbing the big tree, I didn't have to drink milk with every meal as my mother would have insisted, and I could eat ketchup on everything. I did, pouring it over meat, pasta, and vegetables—which did not achieve the desired effect of making green beans any more palatable.

My dad's admission to the hospital did not immediately set off alarms in me. He had been in and out for as long as I could remember. So I was used to being sent to one relative or another for a couple of days, and then, sooner rather than later, everything would be back to the way it was. I hadn't expected this time to be any different. After all, Hodgkin's disease was not fatal, even when they misdiagnosed it, as they had in Dad's case. He would live a long time. I had already worried about that one and had been reassured—by my mother this time—and I could stop doing sit-ups and go to sleep.

Since Mom worked nights, Dad and I were left to our own devices. We spent our evenings listening to his albums of old radio programs, usually mysteries such as *The Shadow*, or watching his favorite TV shows, such as *Taxi* and *WKRP in Cincinnati*. I was in bed early, but I would usually crawl out of bed and down the stairs at midnight when my mom arrived home from work. Often my grandmother would come over with doughnuts, and I rode a sugar high well into the wee hours of the morning.

St. Joseph's hospital was right off iconic Lake Shore Drive, so I was always excited to go and see my dad. It meant that I could peek over at the savage waves of the lake in early October to see if I could spot any sharks. I had been told repeatedly that sharks did not live in Lake Michigan, that they could survive only in the ocean, yet I remained skeptical. The shark in *Jaws* did not seem like the type to let a little thing like salt content in the water get in the way of terrorizing people wherever and whenever he chose. I was obsessed with *Jaws*, having seen snippets of it on the Sunday-night movie before my mother caught me and changed the channel to something more appropriate: *Kojak*.

I remember that, when going up to visit my dad, I'd walk through the lobby past the statue of St. Joseph, moving out of the way of the nuns—Daughters of Charity dressed in their habits with elaborate headpieces, just like Sister Bertrell from the *The Flying Nun*. When a pack of these women would step off the elevator, my mother would whisper to me that that was the kind of nun my grandmother had been before she met my grandpa.

I don't remember much about my visits with Dad at the hospital other than when I would leave, any fears I might have had about his health always seemed silly. He seemed fine to me, and so I reveled in my living arrangements that seemed to change on a daily basis. There was, of course, the week with Aunt Carol. But I couldn't miss too much school, and Highland Park was too far away to commute, and so I returned to the city. I liked the disruption to my schedule; I felt quite exotic going from my grandmother's one night and to my aunt Eileen's another.

In early October I went back to sleeping in my own bed, my aunt Ginger started staying with me, and things seemed as if they were getting back to normal. All we needed was for my dad to come home. It was then that I learned about intensive care. Intensive care was a special room in the hospital where children were not allowed to visit, and so I no longer was able to see my father. There seemed to be some other problem because my mother could not sleep there either, so she had to sleep at home.

Privately, I was glad because I was missing my routine—although I never said it, since I knew from my mom's kohl-rimmed eyes and continuously furrowed brow that this was not the time to make demands on my parents. But the disruption to my schedule was getting old fast. I missed Sunday mornings—jumping into my parents' bed, moving in between them and watching the news before getting dressed and going to Mass. I missed creeping out of bed at midnight to go downstairs and eat doughnuts. I was ready to finish learning how to ride a bicycle, something Dad and I had been working on earlier in the summer. The weather was getting cold, and there was not much time left for bike riding. I was ready for things to go back to normal.

Sleeping at home with Mom, tucked safely in her bed, was a start; now all we needed was for Dad to get better, and we would be back in business. On Friday I arrived home from school and found my grandma smoking a cigarette in the kitchen. Normally, I loved spending time with my grandma, but I knew her presence meant that my mom was at the hospital and that I would probably have to go to her house for the night. I really wanted to sleep in my own bed.

When she saw me, she hugged me tighter than usual and whispered in my ear, "You'll always be my baby." I assented, but as I pulled away she grabbed my hands in hers and said, "Why don't we say a little prayer."

I was used to praying before I went to bed, during Mass, and at CCD, but that was about it. My family did not even say grace before meals except on Thanksgiving, so the idea of praying in the middle of a Friday afternoon struck me as odd, to say the least. There was a pause as my grandma stared at me expectantly. I assumed this was my cue to start, so I began: "Now I lay me down to sleep . . ."

Grandma tossed her head back and laughed. "Why don't we try another one? How about we pray the Hail Mary and ask the Blessed Mother to take extra special care of your daddy?" And so we began. My grandmother's cold, thin hands enveloped mine, and she spoke slowly, as if she couldn't remember the words. I sensed that this was serious prayer—it was the kind of prayer my grandma did when she went to Mass, the kind she did after communion when she buried her face in her hands. I would mimic her, pressing my face into my small palms, but nothing much happened except for seeing flashes of light on the back of my eyelids like I always saw when I rubbed my eyes. I figured I had to wait for my first communion before I would be able to do serious prayer—or maybe it would come when I became a priest like Grandma said I would. I assumed this whole serious-prayer thing was something she had picked up when she was a nun.

We sat together silently at the kitchen table for what felt like an eternity but was probably only about five minutes. My grandpa came in then, a large, easy, free presence. "How ya doin', skeeziks?" He put out his hand and I squeezed it tight. "Ouch, ouch, ouch!" He feigned pain at my grip and then picked me up and carried me into the living room. I wrapped my arms around his neck, grateful for the respite from the prayer and more significantly from the drop in my stomach when he hoisted me into the air. Grandma was making me uneasy with the earnestness of her Hail Marys, and the longer I stayed with her, the less I wanted to—because of what she *wasn't* saying.

The Three Stooges were on and I leapt from Grandpa's arms to the big blue couch. Curly and Larry were making gumbo soup, which they erroneously thought was "gumball" soup, and I laughed hysterically as their high-society guests began to chew and chew and chew on the gumbo, unable to stop and too concerned about appearances to let on that something was wrong.

I loved *The Three Stooges*—Curly especially, who seemed so sweet and gentle. The noises he made and the reactions he had to the world around him were completely relatable to my six-year-old mind. I never liked Moe. He was far too sensible and impatient for my taste. Too much like an adult, too quick to anger at the playfulness and curiosity of Curly. My grandmother was like Moe, acting like a grown-up, taking the world too seriously, and being concerned about things beyond her control.

The rest of that Friday was filled with a blur of *Three Stooges* reruns and Chinese takeout, as my grandpa fell in and out of sleep next to me on the big, blue couch and my grandma chain-smoked and talked in hushed tones on the telephone in the kitchen. I eventually fell asleep in my too small Incredible Hulk pajamas.

"No." It was the only word I could utter, and I did it repeatedly until it became a mantra. I was angry and unable to articulate my situation. This was not supposed to happen. Fathers were supposed to live a long time. I had just started first grade. On my knees, I tried to push the enormous surge of rage out of me by clawing, squeezing, and pummeling the big blue sofa.

Mom wrapped her arms around me and I screamed, "No!" I pulled away from her. Someone had turned off the television; I turned it back on and sat on the floor directly in front of it. Around me, people made phone calls and guests entered and exited. People were crying and trying to say comforting things. Someone brought fried chicken, and all the while I watched television—*The Little Rascals*, *The Three Stooges*, *The Courtship of Eddie's Father*, and *The Brady Bunch*— until the only light in the room came from the cathode tube.

My mother would come by, stroke my dark curls, and ask if I was OK and then tell me I was sitting too close to the television and that it would hurt my eyes. I looked straight ahead. An endless stream of adults came by trying to hug me and tell me that everything would be OK and that my dad was in heaven now.

"Actually, he's not!" I would correct them. "He's in purgatory"—recalling the catechesis my grandmother had given me about the afterlife. "Only the perfect go to heaven; everyone else has to go to purgatory first to get perfect."

Grandmother, my theological guide and spiritual director, had told me all about purgatory as well as heaven and hell. As a priest, I would, of course, go directly to heaven, like all the saints, or firstborn boys in an Irish Catholic household. But most would have to spend time in purgatory before getting the go-ahead to head up to St. Peter.

I imagined purgatory to be a lot like the library, my six-year-old mind equating good behavior with not talking. The space between eternal damnation and the beatific vision would be filled by reading *Curious George Goes to the Hospital* (my standard fare at the children's library), not the worst fate imaginable, but certainly not the greatest either. I pictured my dad in his white T-shirt and mad mop of black curly hair sitting on a wooden chair with all the other denizens of purgatory; reading a book on car maintenance (his favorite subject) while puffing on a cigarette; occasionally looking up to see whether his number had been called, as he did while waiting at the supermarket deli.

Heaven was much easier for me to imagine, since it was quite literally just above the clouds. In the summer after Dad's death, I would often lie on my back and stare up at the sky, imagining the beauty and wonder of heaven going on just past the puffy white ceiling. It proved helpful for me as I imagined my father's time in purgatory to be relatively short; the only sin of his that came to mind was his chain-smoking, and I wasn't even sure that was a sin anymore because I'd recently found out from a CCD teacher that chewing with your mouth open was not a sin, contrary to what my parents said. My entire moral compass had been thrown off kilter with that revelation. So I figured my dad had made it to heaven quickly and was now directly above me, just out of sight, watching over me.

As the theme song to *The Brady Bunch* came up and the comfortingly familiar grid of nine shiny faces came on the screen, I noticed the quiet. The business of the afternoon—the noise and the clomping of feet in and out—had ceased. I turned around and saw my mother seated on the big blue couch, watching me. Her eyes were swollen and her face raw from crying, her body limp with exhaustion. I went over to her and stood in front of her. For a moment neither of us said anything. My mom just stared at me. The pause seemed endless, and I had no words. And then I did.

"Well, I thought they'd never leave," I said.

My mother laughed as I'd never heard her before, loud and clear, as if something had been freed from a long and arduous captivity. She pulled me close; and I curled up next to her; and together, alone in the big old house, we watched *The Brady Bunch*.

Smells like Holy Spirit

The tap on the shoulder startled me in the midst of my shenanigans. It was followed by a sharp, stern "That'll be enough of that." Roxanne Pticek and Lisa Slowinski looked at each other and started giggling. I was humiliated.

I was trying to put on a show, and Mr. Pticek—Roxanne's father and our CCD teacher—was not particularly supportive of my aspirations. Granted, we were in church, for a CCD prayer service or something. But really, who paid attention to those things, especially in the eighth grade? I don't remember exactly what I was doing in my vain attempts to make Roxanne and Lisa laugh, some sort of clowning with my ski cap. Whatever it was I do remember that it wasn't my best material.

The scenario wasn't new. I was reprimanded frequently for joking around and talking when I wasn't supposed to. But this particular moment stands out primarily because it was when I stopped believing in God.

I don't think Mr. Pticek's reprimand had much to do with my decision, although I'm sure my feelings of embarrassment and anger in the moment might have precipitated things. Forced to stand still and pay attention, it occurred to me that I might not actually believe what I was hearing.

Since my father's death, I had become, by turns, the class clown and the angriest kid in the world. My mother had remarried, and with the new marriage had come a new home on the other side of the city with a new school and a new baby sister. It would take me a while to warm up to all these things—and by "while" I mean seven to thirteen years.

School and I had always had a love-hate relationship. I loved the social component of school and hated the work. I wasn't one of those geniuses who didn't have to study and could get all As, but I didn't have to do a heck of a lot to get Bs and Cs, which was fine with me. Unfortunately, it was not OK with my parents or my teachers. I heard a lot of, "You could be getting As if you just applied yourself," to which I always thought, *Yeah, I could, but applying myself would interfere with my social life, especially during school.*

I had a lot of social fish to fry during the day, and paying attention in class and doing work would interfere with such important matters as note passing ("Melissa, do you like me? Check Y or N. If you check N, don't tell *anyone* about this note, OK?"), playwriting (well, it was actually just a word-for-word transcription of *Saved by the Bell* episodes done from memory, courtesy of numerous viewings), and making fun of my teachers and all classroom content ("Today we will learn about Lake Titicaca!" Lake Titicaca jokes are comedy gold in the fifth grade).

So as you can see, my plate was quite full during the school day, so learning and listening were hard to fit in to my already-hectic schedule. Not shockingly, my teachers were completely unsupportive and were never open to "working" around my schedule, in spite of my protestations for some sort of "compromise."

Both sides were pretty unwavering in their commitments to their respective agendas, and I wound up being in trouble a lot. I probably would have been better off had I learned just to accept the consequences of my behavior, but I was an angry kid who also watched a lot of television. It was a perfect storm.

This was the era of the "very special episode," wherein once or twice a season, a sitcom would switch gears and move away from the standard lightweight high jinks and focus on a particularly relevant topic of the moment, ripped from the headlines, as it were. These rarely involved one of the main characters on the show but instead focused on a special guest-starring friend and/or relative—such as Tom Hanks in the role of alcoholic Uncle Ned on a very special episode of *Family Ties*. Using an outside character saved the writers from having to follow up on the issue in subsequent episodes.

While there were certain aspects of the very special episode that I wasn't fond of (namely, the drama, because it took away the laughs), there were parts I enjoyed (namely, the drama, because it gave me behavior to model poorly and inappropriately).

So when I was reprimanded in school for my behavior, more often than not I made like Tom Hanks as Uncle Ned after being confronted by Meredith Baxter-Birney and Michael J. Fox about his drinking, and stormed out. This wasn't healthy behavior for Tom Hanks as Uncle Ned in the Keaton family kitchen, nor was it healthy behavior for me in Miss Hamilton's fourth-grade classroom.

Uncle Ned eventually got help. I usually found myself two blocks away from school and realizing that my mother would kill me if I showed up at home at eleven thirty on a Tuesday morning. I returned to school, chin held high as if I had somehow proved my point.

It was inevitable that I landed in the office of the school therapist. According to the therapist, I was apparently still angry over my father's death. I begged to disagree. I believed I was angry because my teachers wouldn't let me talk in class, because Jamie Bougher wouldn't tell me what happened on *The A-Team* when we were in line for the bathroom, and because my mom made me peanut butter and jelly sandwiches on wheat bread and not white bread like the cool kids had. This therapist didn't get it at all.

I pretty much lied the entire time I spent with the therapist. I made up stories about my weekends, usually involving fantasies that revolved around going to restaurants by myself and ordering a steak dinner with a limestone salad (limestone salads seemed really grown-up), or of smoking cigarettes and going to the bank by myself and checking on my stocks and bonds (I really had no idea). In retrospect I can see that the therapist knew I was lying and probably didn't believe that a nine-year-old boy was frequenting honky-tonk bars and riding mechanical bulls (*Urban Cowboy* was the Sunday-night movie that week), and more than likely she was just indulging my fantasies.

In spite of my juvenile delinquencies, I wanted to be a priest. It seemed like a good gig: I would have to work only on Sundays (and Saturday evenings), and I already had the Mass memorized. My grandma taught me how to say the rosary, and I loved it; so when I told her that I wanted to be a priest, she didn't hide her delight. "You'll be my priest," she uttered triumphantly, finally getting the religious vocation that a first-generation Irish with five daughters, one son, and eight grandchildren had come to expect.

She had been a nun, herself, momentarily. "I could have had three hots and a cot," she would say in the more difficult moments of child rearing, alluding to the year she spent as a postulant with the Daughters of Charity in St. Louis. That she was a Daughter of Charity was of particular interest to me because that was the religious order that wore the cornet head-piece as a part of their habit, the same headpiece worn by Sister Bertrille on *The Flying Nun*. Since the cornet was the device that catapulted a young Sally Field into the air each episode, I had lots of questions about it for my grandma. Her response was always the same, "You know that TV is not real don't you, Jacob?" I didn't know.

My childhood happened to coincide with the rise of the family-centered situation comedy; shows about the nuclear family pervaded the airwaves in the early to mid-1980s. The family-sitcom boom commenced with *The Cosby Show*, which became an unprecedented hit, and continued with shows such as *Family Ties*, *Growing Pains*, and *Mr. Belvedere*. Along with these came a slew of series centered on the nontraditional family unit, such as *Kate & Allie*, *Who's the Boss?* and *Full House*. In the 1980s, television was all about the family, and I was seated front and center.

These televised families, with all of their foibles and mishaps, gave me a sense of serenity and security in my own very topsy-turvy existence. There was something incredibly soothing about watching problems being solved in twenty-two minutes, about a living room without a fourth wall, about bright warm lights and a laugh track underscoring every one-liner.

On these shows, nobody's father died, and if a parent did happen to die—as happened to the mother on *The Hogan Family*—the grief ended by the twenty-second minute, never to be acknowledged again.

These shows not only were comforting and consoling but also were in their own way affirming. I loved reruns but could never understand the appeal of the sitcoms of the 1950s and 1960s, which idealized the family. Granted, the families on *The Cosby Show* and *Family Ties* were hardly realistic, but they did celebrate the fundamentally flawed nature of their characters and humanized the family unit in ways shows such as *Leave It to Beaver*, *My Three Sons*, and *Make Room for Daddy* never did. They showed parents losing their tempers, making mistakes, and sometimes tiring of their role. The kids faced real-life issues dealing with drugs, sex, and failure—and this ultimately set the stage for the most unflinching look at the American family that television had ever seen.

When *Roseanne* debuted in the fall of 1988, it was a revelation. Based on the stand-up act of Roseanne Barr, the show followed the adventures of the blue-collar Connor family and their friends in fictional Lanford, Illinois. Dan and Roseanne

Connor, loosely based on Barr and her then husband Bill Pentland, were hardly the witty and attractive Cliff and Claire Huxtable of *Cosby* fame, let alone Ward and June Cleaver. Dan and Roseanne were overweight, often unemployed, struggling from week to week to make ends meet. Sometimes they snapped at their kids or didn't clean the house. Often, they yelled at each other.

Their three children—Becky, Darlene, and DJ—were surly, uncooperative, and combative, sometimes with their parents, always with one another. It was as authentic a representation of family dynamics as was ever shown on television, and because of this (not in spite of) it was phenomenally funny.

The humor lay in the identification with the Connor clan; audiences recognized the imperfections and frailties of Dan and Roseanne because they didn't so much try to maintain an ideal as they tried to keep themselves afloat. Bills needed to be paid, food needed to get on the table, and the kids needed to be cared for; there was little time for the indulgences found in other family-related shows.

The show was originally titled *Life and Stuff,* but the title was changed at the last minute as a result of its creator and star's rapidly ascending public persona. Yet the original title was right on the money; the show was about life for better and for worse. It was unflinching in its examination of all things family, however taboo the subject may have seemed, and it did so with thoughtfulness, care, and humor.

The sitcom has always been an unloved and underappreciated genre, a necessary evil of network television. The appeal to programmers lies in its relatively cheap overhead; the format historically utilizes only one or two sets in a studio and a cast of five or six actors. Compared to most hour-long dramas, which require the much more expensive location shooting (whatever the location, it is always more expensive to work outside of the controlled and convenient environment of a studio soundstage) as well as a cast of ten to twelve actors, on top of a longer production schedule.

Dramas receive the prestige, and sitcoms make the money. This is not at all out of line with the general view of Hollywood at large. In the eighty-some-year history of the Academy Awards, only a handful of comedies have won for Best Picture. Hollywood's understanding of art can be at best described as myopic, particularly when some of its most memorable and groundbreaking moments have come courtesy of the comic medium.

Because of its rigid structural layout, the sitcom presents a rather benign facade. Yet because the parameters of its form have been so clearly delineated, the sitcom can offer a paradoxical freedom and artistic license to its creators that other media cannot.

Roseanne pushed the boundaries of comedy without ever moving beyond the structural conventions of the sitcom, which had been calcified for decades. It was what occurred within the traditional sitcom structure—an opening teaser; two acts; an A story (or primary story), B story (secondary), and sometimes C story (tertiary story), also called the runner—that irrevocably changed the picture of the American family on television.

Ironically, the only thing that the folks behind *Roseanne* did was tell the truth. They showed an American family, like so many other American families, just trying to live, with all the breaking, shouting, and loving that occurs in a house full of kids. This wasn't Cliff and Claire Huxtable, a doctor and lawyer, respectively, in their posh Brooklyn Heights brownstone. Nor was it Mike and Carol Brady, he an architect, she a stay-at-home mom (with a live-in maid, no less!) in suburban Los Angeles. This was Dan and Roseanne Connor, a self-employed drywall installer and his wife who bounced from minimum-wage job to minimum-wage job in small town, blue-collar Lanford, Illinois, where everybody knows everybody and nobody is going anywhere.

Wrapped in a blanket, with two pairs of socks on my feet, in our perpetually arctic house—thanks to my parents' staunch conviction that using central heating was wasteful, especially with so many sweatshirts, socks, and blankets at hand—I could identify with the characters on *Roseanne* in a way I couldn't with other shows. Those shows were fantasy, a look at a privileged and idyllic world that I did not belong to.

On *Roseanne*, I watched eldest daughter Becky beg her parents not to acknowledge her during a night out at the bowling alley, sneak into her parent's liquor cabinet with a friend and proceed to get drunk, and have a parent walk in on her while she danced with headphones on in her bedroom. I watched Darlene, the middle child, blame her little brother for a low grade at school because he destroyed her last-minute, rush-job, extra-credit project; baffle her parents in puberty by her sudden disinterest in absolutely everything; and try to forge her parent's signature on a bad report card. I watched Dan and Roseanne argue over the best way to discipline their children, over Dan not doing enough around the house, and over Roseanne's omnipresent family.

All of these moments paralleled my own life, and I appreciated the Connor family because of their bruises and because they weren't afraid to show them. Here was a family that was far from perfect, and yet this did not make them contemptible or pitiful, as was usually the case in the black-and-white world of television. Here was a family that was neither shiny nor corrupt; this was a nuanced, deeply affecting essaying of the American family.

What drove that authenticity was the love simmering just beneath the surface of every moment of each scene. While Roseanne's acting abilities may be questionable at best, she was smart enough to surround herself with some of the most talented actors of her own or any generation. One of the key components of an excellent actor is his or her ability to raise the level of those around them, and that is just what John Goodman and Laurie Metcalf were able to do.

Goodman was exceptional in his role as the oft-encumbered but never defeated Dan Connor. In a role that easily could have disappeared into the shadow of his cacophonous costar, Goodman created a wonderfully blustering, burly lunk of a hero—the thinking man's Ralph Kramden. Dan frequently lost his temper, vegetated in front of the television, and overindulged in food and drink. Yet never for an instant did the audience doubt his love and fealty for his family.

He was an especially attentive husband who made up for his occasional moments of male obliviousness with tender gestures of affection and gallantry. He encouraged his wife in her own interests, including preparing a space in the basement for her to write, free from the incessant demands of the children. He teased, wrestled, and tackled his wife with the sweetest abandon and left little doubt that he was just as crazy about her fifteen years into their marriage as he was on the first day.

This is a testament to Goodman's acting ability. Acting is all in the details, and each episode provided new opportunities for Goodman to add more layers to the character of Dan as well as fresh charges of comedic spark to his on-screen relationship with Roseanne. When Roseanne asked Dan to fix the sink, it was not enough to just respond in kind. Instead, Dan responded, "Yes, dear" in the cartoonish voice of the henpecked husband, his head shaking sheepishly in mock resignation, a good natured gibe at his wife's domestic victory.

Indeed, most exchanges between Dan and Roseanne had the same color, with Goodman in particular able to conjure the extraordinary out of the ordinary. *Roseanne* was made up of these moments, simple moments of pure joy—those moments we all experience at the most unexpected of times: washing the dishes, driving to the supermarket, eating breakfast. These moments when God takes a snapshot of us, fully engaged, fully alive, loving and laughing with those around us.

Roseanne was cathartic for me in a way that, at the time, I could not comprehend. I saw the Connors with their warts and all and recognized my own life right there. They were not sad or pathetic; they were enjoying their lives in spite of their adversities. This made sense to me. I had learned very early that life didn't always work out as you expected it to, that sometimes things went awry, but that didn't mean that you stopped moving.

I think that was where the disconnect between myself and my teachers came in. One of the most frustrating things about my school experience was the treatment I received from them once they discovered that my father had passed away. I knew that they meant well, but I also knew that they didn't know what to do with this extraordinarily angry boy. There were a lot of understanding looks and sad faces, as if I should be wearing sackcloth and ashes, and I felt as if they expected me to be sad all the time.

"How was your weekend?" they would ask, as if I spent the whole weekend sobbing in bed, or if I didn't, I should have. But I didn't want that—I wanted to laugh and enjoy myself and enjoy my life. I was too young to understand why I was so angry, but I did understand that life kept happening whether you wanted it to or not.

I was angry with my teachers because the help they were offering wasn't the help I needed or wanted. I was angry because I could sense that they didn't know what to do with me, but in reality, I didn't know what to do with them either. They wanted me to behave like Oliver Twist. I wanted something that I couldn't articulate—I just knew it wasn't pity.

I have wondered frequently whether I would have been a better student had my father not died. I doubt it; I am fundamentally not organized and would have lacked the self-awareness to recognize that just because I'm not fascinated by something doesn't mean I shouldn't pay attention. That's the sort of revelation that can come only with growth and experience.

What I do realize now is that from the time my father passed when I was six years old to the moment in church as a thirteen-year-old when I stopped believing in God, a lot had changed in me. As I stood there, angry at Mr. Pticek for humiliating me in front of Roxanne and Lisa, angry at my parents for forcing me to go to CCD, and angry at God for pulling the rug out from under me, I decided then and there that I'd had enough. As far as I was concerned, God was dead.

I'll Be Here All
Week—Try the Veal!

It was Holy Thursday—more important, it was the day before spring break. The bell for sixth period had just rung, as the lot of glandular teenage boys tumbled into Brother Mahoney's sophomore English class. With our skinny neckties—it was the 1980s—twisted into close and not-so-close approximations of Windsor knots and hung from our damp necks, we sweated our way through the final few class periods before our ten-day furlough.

Brother Mahoney was an egret of a man: thin, pointy, and snappish. He was all sharp elbows and bulging eyes as he passed out a pop quiz, moving from row to row of smelly, sticky adolescent boys. His pinching hands swiped out sheets of text with irascible efficiency. A soft, barely audible breeze of lamentation cooled the room. It was the day before spring break—what kind of monster gave a pop quiz on *Julius Caesar* the day before spring break? Of course, most of us knew better than to utter our dissatisfaction aloud.

Brother Mahoney was prickly as a hedgehog and prone to emaciated fits of rage at any given time. We tread lightly around him. This was, after all, a few years prior to the news breaking of sex abuse in the church, so there was still a definite sense of infallibility when it came to members of the clergy, and even more so because this was the South Side of Chicago in the late 1980s: our parish was very much a holdover from the 1950s. The majority of my classmates were the sons of cops and firefighters, and the prevailing mentality among the parents of my classmates was that if we were hit by a teacher or other authority figure, we probably deserved it.

Kevin O'Brien sat directly in front of me, but it might as well have been forty miles away for all that we knew of each other. Kevin was a class clown of a sort, and by that I mean that he was of the sort of class clown that wasn't really funny, just disruptive. Kevin and I were in a majority of classes together, but the only thing I knew about him was that he took great pleasure in discovering people's vulnerabilities and then harassing them incessantly until he grew bored and found someone newer, fresher, and weaker. So I pretty much tried to stay out of his way. He would occasionally note my propensity for wearing sweaters daily even in the most oppressive heat—due solely to my inability to attain a proper length for my tie—and would occasionally give me grief for it, but for the most part I was small change. I kept my mouth shut and stayed out of his way.

As Brother Mahoney made his way over to our row, Kevin boldly and stupidly piped up, "You can't give us a pop quiz; it's the day before spring break!"

I automatically flinched and turned my head away, my eyelids fluttering in terror. Brother Mahoney snapped—make that, "Brother Mahoney snapped again."

"I think I'm a better judge of that than you are, you little a_____," he screeched and flew over and began slapping Kevin repeatedly with both bony hands. He was scrawny rage in motion, like one of those dancing Day of the Dead skeletons, arms and legs flying every which way.

The rest of the class looked on in horror, which quickly turned into discomfort as it became abundantly clear that Brother was not hurting Kevin in the slightest and that Kevin was, in fact, politely sitting and accepting the blows with no resistance, embarrassed by their feebleness but respectful of Brother's authority. When the limp battering had ended after an uncomfortable minute or so, we all quietly went about taking our quizzes. Just another day at Catholic school.

The all-boys Catholic school was a big change for me because I had been strictly a public school kid up to high school. But my mother had recently watched a *20/20* investigation about the satanic cult phenomenon sweeping the nation's public high schools and decided that I was ripe for the picking on the basis of my recent reluctance to go to Mass on Sunday morning. "You've always been so easily suggestible," she said as she wrote down the name of a new liquid diet on the piece of scrap paper she always kept handy while watching *Oprah*—in order to write down the latest life-changing product her mentor deigned to share with her minions.

"You're very naive, Jacob," she said, using my full first name, which meant she was all business.

"Remember how you thought that you had to use two separate bowls for wet and dry ingredients when making cookies?" she said, while sipping a can of Pepsi Clear.

I nodded in agreement, although I was a bit confused. My mother had taught me many things, and I had little doubt that I had a lot more to learn about the adversity life had to offer, yet I did not quite understand the analogous relationship my mother continually drew between my not knowing that I did not need to follow the directions regarding wet and dry bowls in a cookie recipe and her concern about me joining a cult, satanic or otherwise.

"I think its best that you go to St. Laurence," she said. And that is the story of how my mother saved me from joining a cult—oh, wait.

I survived high school without any bruises, thanks primarily to having learned to keep my head down and my mouth closed. I was no longer the social gadfly I had been in elementary school. There was a different set of rules at an all-boys school, with a different hierarchy. Sports were king, and my sport was tennis—not the sport that was going to win you fame and prestige in a blue-collar neighborhood on the South Side of Chicago.

My time at St. Laurence did nothing to improve my relationship with God; in fact, it affirmed the doubts I already had. The erratic behavior of many of the brothers and the hypocrisy that manifested itself in the school administration soured me on organized religion and God. Not that I wasn't ripe for the picking.

For the first time in my life, I didn't have a lot of friends, so I wound up spending my Saturday nights with my old familiar friend, *Saturday Night Live*. This was the era of the first renaissance of the show. After the initial glory days of the first cast, the show went into a rapid decline in the early 1980s with the departure of Lorne Michaels and was, several times, on the verge of cancellation. Michaels eventually returned, and the show began to slowly but surely build itself back up.

For me, this was the golden era during which my understanding of the jokes and sketches developed. "Weekend Update" was no longer a chore to sit through while waiting for the following sketch. Dennis Miller seemed to my teenage mind too cool for school. His hip, sardonic rants and oh-so-eighties hair turned "Update" into one of my favorite parts of the show. Miller's commentary also brought out a level of concern about the world around me that had never manifested before. Suddenly, politics was interesting to me; what was going on outside my immediate surroundings seemed to matter. I began to see that it was important to be informed, to make informed choices, and to recognize that I could take actions that would affect the world around me.

The show featured an all-star cast: Jon Lovitz, Jan Hooks, later Mike Myers, and of course Phil Hartman. Hartman was my favorite. From the anal-retentive chef to Frank Sinatra and Ed McMahon, everything he did made me laugh. His over-the-top approach and absurdist sensibility were completely in line with what I considered funny. Hartman's Sinatra wasn't nearly as accurate an impersonation as Joe Piscopo's, but it was a lot funnier. Hartman chose one or two traits that defined a character and hit them for all they were worth. He recognized that what was funny was not so much the accuracy of our behavior, but the absurd levels to which we can take our actions. Piscopo went for accuracy, Hartman for absurdity, and he was the better comedian for it.

Saturday Night Live got me through the weekends, and David Letterman got me through the week. This was in the days when Dave was still on after Johnny Carson. He was still the bad boy of NBC and the heir apparent to Johnny's slot. Things change.

I'll admit that I have never watched a full episode of Dave's show since he moved into the earlier timeslot on CBS. I've always held that Letterman is at his best an hour after mainstream. The late-night slot suited him and his humor, so reliant as it is on overturning sacred cows. Letterman never batted an eye with a celebrity and never went out of his way to make any of them feel comfortable—a nice change of pace from the softball lovefest that occurred an hour earlier with Johnny and now Leno. They are that kind of comic: good hosts, with a gentle, nonthreatening kind of humor. Letterman, at his peak, needs teeth for his humor.

I spent my high school years in front of the television. My grades improved, and so did my behavior. Not even realizing what I was preparing myself for, with no real aspirations to be a comedian, I spent all my free time studying comedy. I pored over any book I could find about *Saturday Night Live* or any other comedy show. There was really no great plan; I just wanted to laugh.

Eventually, I headed for college, where my major was the obvious choice for anyone whose sole interests were watching television and reading about comedy: accounting.

I always admired accountants, ever since I had seen those *Look Who's Talking* movies—you know, the ones with Kirstie

Alley and John Travolta and the talking babies. Actually, the babies didn't talk, but you could hear their thoughts, and the voices in their head sounded like Bruce Willis and Joan Rivers. Well Kirstie Alley's character in the movie was a certified public accountant, and it seemed like a great job. She really seemed to enjoy it, and I liked the idea of being organized the way accountants are.

A friend of mine recently pointed out to me that we often admire and are attracted to those people whose skill sets are in opposition to our own. They represent something we wished we had.

My response was, "Where were you when I was applying to college for accounting?"

I learned very quickly that I had no affinity or interest in accounting, and as fast as you can say, "I just skipped three straight weeks of classes in Econ 120," I was on the hunt for a different major.

As it turned out, I hadn't learned my lesson particularly well and decided that, given my love for the classic 1980s hit series *L.A. Law*, being an attorney was my true calling. But law school was a ways off, as I had yet to complete my undergraduate degree. Not accidentally, the majority of classes I took in school were theater classes, and since I could've sworn that somebody once told me (most likely myself) that a theater major was a good degree to have for law school, I bit the bullet and got my degree.

I met Josh in one of my acting classes. I hated him at first sight. He was nineteen years old and a stand-up comedian and seemed to fit every negative stereotype I had about stand-up comedians. He was always "on," continually doing "bits" as they say, and he never stopped talking. He drove me crazy. I was trying to be a serious actor-lawyer, and this guy had no respect for the craft. Add to that, the teachers all loved him; he had an ease and confidence onstage that I definitely lacked.

We were assigned to work together on a project for class, *A Raisin in the Sun*. Who better to explore the plight of the working-class African American family in the 1950s than an Irish Catholic and a Jew in 1998? It was within the context of our shared misery over the complete inappropriateness of our casting that we became friends.

After we completed our piece in front of our horrified classmates, we sat down to receive notes from our director. While I don't recall many of the notes I received that day, I do recall one being something along the lines of "perhaps you should have considered wearing makeup to make yourself more believable." Yep, that's right. It was suggested in Chicago in 1998, and not Mississippi in 1847, that I would've been more believable as a black man had I worn blackface.

After our debacle of a project, Josh and I did what any self-respecting college students would do after performing an all-white production of *A Raisin in the Sun*: we got drunk. Laughing over the absurdity of the situation, Josh told me that he thought I was funny and should try my hand at comedy. Up to that point, I had nothing but disdain for Josh and felt that his humor was utterly sophomoric. However, sitting and listening to Josh carry on about my comedic gifts, it occurred to me that perhaps I had underestimated Josh's taste in humor.

Josh was dating a woman who was a performer at the Second City; in fact she had been brought in to replace an actress who had just been hired as a writer by *Saturday Night*

Live, a woman by the name of Tina Fey. Josh began inviting me to hang out with his girlfriend and her comedy friends, and I was hooked.

That summer, Josh and I took an improv class, and quickly my whole world became all about comedy: following Josh around the city to his various stand-up gigs and getting the opportunity to hang out with the folks at the Second City at the tavern across the street from the theater after the show. I was just a hanger-on—the friend of the boyfriend, as it were—and I spent most of my time with my mouth shut, sitting and listening, sipping my beer, as these comedic geniuses went to town with one another, exchanging bits and discussing the nuances and structure of comedy. It was fascinating stuff for a kid just starting out, surrounded by such brilliant folks.

I never thought of comedy as having a structure of any sort. I thought it was just something that you did or something that you were: you were either funny or you were not. I didn't realize that a lot of variables went into making something funny: premise, rhythm, status, delivery. Comedy—real comedy, that is, the kind that people got paid to do—was serious business and didn't come easy. While some people have a natural gift, a lot of work is required to develop and build on that gift in order to achieve success.

The wisdom I was taking in on late nights in the smoky confines of city taverns was being put to good use in my improv classes. Improvisation was a revelation for me. Acting without a script, performing wild and outrageous characters of my own making on the spot, felt right for me in a way that nothing else ever had. Other people seemed to be terrified of going up onstage without a net—no script, no props, no costume. But for me all of it seemed just right. I could create my own world, any world I wanted, and include my own characters based on various people in my life, something I had been doing privately for years. Now I had a public audience, and they laughed. They laughed a lot.

I didn't realize it at the time, but I was experiencing what St. Ignatius called consolation. It was not about the high that I received while performing (which did happen on occasion) but about the "rightness" I felt while I was doing it; there was an ease, a comfort I felt, not just while performing but afterward as well. This interior feeling of soundness and ease was God's way of confirming for me that I was on the right path, something I had never felt in anything else I had done up to that point.

But "God" wasn't a part of the equation for me then. I was a self-proclaimed atheist, or agnostic, depending on how lucky I felt on a given day. Yet for some reason I found myself praying frequently, usually before a performance or before a plane took off. After the show, or when the plane landed safely, I attributed my heartfelt pleas for peace and safety to superstition.

Had I been truly honest with myself at the time, I would've been able to acknowledge that it wasn't so much that I didn't believe in God as that I didn't find God to be particularly convenient.

Going to Mass on Sunday would've meant, well, getting out of bed on Sunday. My parents had insisted that I attend Mass weekly until I turned eighteen, and the moment I did, I stopped. God was an obstacle that did not fit in with the rest of my plans, which were having a good time Saturday night and sleeping in on Sunday mornings.

I shut God out; it was easier than dealing with the reality of the situation, which was that I was still very angry about my father's death. I told myself that I didn't believe. I gave myself the standard arguments that believing went contrary to science and that educated people like me didn't believe in things like God. Where was the proof?

Still there were moments, flashes of desire, a yearning for something larger than myself and the world of ego and chaos that I inhabited. I would find myself walking past St. Alphonsus, the church in my neighborhood, and catch myself staring. One Tuesday afternoon, I walked up the staircase. I went to the door and pulled. It was locked. I took that as a sign.

I started getting invitations to perform my comedy. The first classes I had taken were at the Annoyance Theater, located right down the street from Wrigley Field. The Annoyance was founded by three college friends from Indiana, one of whom—Mick Napier—had become the acknowledged master of improvisation in Chicago. As well as being the cofounder and creative head at the Annoyance, Mick was also the artistic director at the Second City. He was responsible for directing some of the most critically acclaimed shows the theater produced in the 1990s, shows that provided springboards for performers such as Tina Fey, Rachel Dratch, and Scott Adsit. Everybody took classes at the Annoyance for the chance to take a class with Mick. But first you had to take a class with Mark.

Mark was one of the three cofounders of Annoyance. He taught the beginning-level improv class and was the antithesis of the traditional comedian. As a performance field, comedy is incredibly macho and competitive. The combination of sharp wit, machismo, and competitiveness does not make for the most nurturing of environments. It can be a tough world to reside in, and it takes a very thick skin to survive in. Mark was unique in that he was a very gentle, kind, and supportive instructor.

Mark put up the front of being a real "guy's guy"; he loved sports and women. But he cried easily and always looked out for the people he cared about. I was a pretty naive kid when I entered improv; I had led a relatively sheltered life, happy as I was in front of the television. Mark looked out for me and helped me. He cast me in shows and always made sure that I was OK.

During class when I was doing a scene, Mark laughed a lot. His laughter meant a lot to me because it was the first time that someone whom I respected for his or her comedy acumen laughed at my work. Eventually, when I moved on to Mick's class, he laughed, too. There was something I had that just might work. My future seemed to be right before me; *Saturday Night Live* didn't seem that far away. I knew where I was headed. How wrong I was.

6

Jokers to the Right

I couldn't see a thing. I walked onto the small stage, hands stretched out in front of me, fingers reaching for any unseen obstacles that could cause me harm. I found my place and moved into position. We were in a "blackout," the moment right before the lights go up and the show begins.

As I stood for a brief moment in the darkness, awaiting the lights, I began to make out shapes before me—the audience, within inches of me, close enough to almost touch. Then one of the shapes started slowly shifting. I heard a slight sniffle, which quickly fused into a mumble, and then a guffaw. The shape was shaking now, and it quickly exploded into full-blown laughter. The lights had not gone up yet. My cast mates and I were still frozen in our opening tableau, awaiting the lights, and this shape—no, this woman; no, *my mother*—was cackling hysterically.

Afterward, standing by the enormous black-and-white photos of John Belushi, Bill Murray, Tina Fey, and the hundreds of other legends who had graced the stages of the Second City, I asked my mother what had been so funny that she had started laughing even before the show had begun.

"I don't know. I just saw you and I knew I was supposed to laugh and I guess I just jumped the gun."

A mother's love is a remarkable thing. Her support knows no bounds. It reminded me of when I was a kid and would play in tennis tournaments. All the other kids' parents would be pressed up against the fence of the courts, shouting support and instructions, and I would look and look for my mom and never find her.

Afterward I would ask her where she was during the match.

"Didn't you see me? I was behind the tree watching with my eyes closed. I get too nervous."

I was grateful for my mother's cockeyed, low-key support.

"I just want you to be happy," she would say whenever I came to her with my latest all-encompassing life plan. And those weren't just words; she meant it. She was just as sincere when I said it as a seven-year-old and told her I wanted to move to Hazzard County, Georgia, and live in Uncle Jessie's barn while thwarting the plots of Boss Hogg along with Bo and Luke Duke as she was when I finished college and told her I wanted to pursue a career in comedy.

When I decided to become a Jesuit, people often would ask me in hushed tones, as if speaking of a death in the family, if my parents were OK with my joining the Jesuits. I was always surprised by this question, as it never occurred to me that they would not be supportive. "Are you kidding me? I'm a comedian. Becoming a Jesuit, with a guaranteed roof over my head and three square meals a day is like being named the CEO of Microsoft by comparison."

So I had my parents' full support after graduating college when I moved into a basement apartment and began life as a comedian, which first and foremost meant getting a day job. There wasn't a lot of money to be had in the world of improv and sketch comedy. Even the ones who had "made it"—that is, the lucky twelve people hired to perform on one of the Second City's two resident stages—were still making very little money. In fact, the goal of being a comedian in Chicago became pretty clear pretty quickly: to get out of Chicago.

Chicago was the place to build a résumé, get a union card, and then get to a coast (either coast) as soon as you could. The Second City had name value, which could maybe—and this was a huge maybe—open some doors for you once you got out to New York or Los Angeles. The best-case scenario was that you were spotted by a scout for *Saturday Night Live*—when they came out once a year to check out the talent pool in Chicago—and were whisked out to New York for an audition and hired on the spot.

But more often than not, what happened was that after a decade or so of doing everything that was possible to do in Chicago, comedywise, a comic would pack up and move out west (or east)—if they were lucky, with a Screen Actors Guild card in tow—and do exactly what he or she had been doing in Chicago: auditioning, doing improv shows for little or no money, hoping, and waiting. And by waiting, I mean waiting . . . tables.

I worked at a coffeehouse my first summer out of college, and I'd like to say that there is a special place in hell reserved for people who think that it's OK to give servers a hard time. I was a horrible server, there is no doubt about it, and I cannot multitask to save my life. As I write this book, literally my whole life has shut down. I am surrounded by coffee mugs, empty water bottles, and books. My superior knocks on my door every couple of weeks to make sure I'm alive. I cannot do more than one thing at a time. I can barely do one thing, except sleep. That, to paraphrase Ralph Wiggum from *The Simpsons* is where I really shine. But seriously, I'm amazed that I can put fork to mouth at this point.

So no, I was not a good server; therefore, I tip my hat to those who can do it well. To be friendly and polite to perfect strangers, all the while managing to keep tabs on eight other groups of perfect strangers and all of their dining needs, is no easy task.

For whatever reason some people like to take out their aggressions and problems in life on food servers, which is utterly unfair since you know they cannot fight back, as their whole income is entirely dependent on making their customer happy. But I would see people bully servers time and again—and no I'm not talking about myself; I was horrible and would be nasty right back, which is why my career at waiting was relatively brief—preying on the weak and the powerless because they could. There, enough of that rant. I feel better now.

Ultimately, I left the world of the service industry to make my fortune doing a very famous show for very little money. I will not name said show for fear of legal repercussions, but suffice to say, it was not the dream job and step to stardom I thought it would be. I had to work long hours with some good people and some not-so-great people. After a while, everything got old and the work developed a definite clock-punching component.

What I discovered in my brief tenure at said famous show was that show business was like every other business but with worse hours—and I would guess more narcotics, although I could be wrong about that. Plus, you usually have to work holidays.

I left the show when I realized that I probably would end up doing it for another decade if I wasn't paying attention, as many in the show already seemed to be doing. This did not appear to be my ticket to *Saturday Night Live* and stardom. And the comedy I was doing in this show was not respected in the same way as the material being done at the Second City, iO (or ImprovOlympic as it was called back then), and the Annoyance Theater. The really good, smart, and cutting-edge comedy developed in those venues.

A lot is always happening in the world of Chicago improv, and when I was starting out it, was no different; people such as Rachel Dratch, Horatio Sanz, and Jason Sudeikis were still quite visible presences in the community. Tina Fey and Amy Poehler had left for the East Coast not long before, and their impact continued to register throughout the city, even as they made names for themselves on a national level.

In the midst of all this, I became roommates with Rick, a friend of my college pal Josh, who had already decided to head for greener pastures in LA. Recently, Rick had left the Second City, where he'd been working on and off for nearly a decade. He was trying to find his way in the world of stand-up, all the while making the inevitable transition toward the coast.

Which coast he was not certain of, but a coast was clearly coming into focus. Rick, like many before him and many after, was attempting to alleviate his decision-making process by submitting writing to all the major comedy shows in the hopes of being hired as a writer. He had already been flown out for a screen test at *Saturday Night Live* a few years before with no success, but now he was counting on writing as his ticket out.

Rick became a mentor to me in a chain-smoking, beer-drinking way that only comedy could allow. I copied everything about him, including vainly attempting to copy his speech patterns, which were equal parts Groucho Marx and Woody Allen. We would sit in our apartment—because we were broke—trading bits while Rick taught me what he called "the math of comedy."

Rick introduced me to comedians such as Lenny Bruce, Nichols and May, and Jonathan Winters. Rick had an edge to him like no one I'd met before. He never went to college, was hired by the Second City at age nineteen, and had been supporting himself through comedy ever since. Like me, he was young when his father died, and he coined us "The Dead Dad's Club," which, macabre as it was, gave me a sense of kinship with him. This was a nice contrast from the isolation I'd felt as the only kid whose dad had died.

The apartment we lived in had been a rotating door for comedians through the years. It was dirt cheap and in a very nice neighborhood close to all the important theaters. There were three bedrooms, and in any given year one or two people were moving out, on to bigger and better things. For instance, the woman who sublet her space to me had left to travel for a year in the Oscar Mayer Wienermobile, sojourning across the

United States on the dime of Oscar Mayer, in a car shaped like a gigantic hot dog. Livin' the dream.

Rick moved in when Josh headed out to LA, and he brought his cat with him. Professor Paws was none too pleased with her new residence, and she made her displeasure known all over our sofa. Soon the apartment reeked of cat urine, stale cigarette smoke, beer, and Febreeze, which I sprayed everywhere, ever hopeful.

I was living the life of the young comic: late nights and bleak mornings. A part of me was having the time of my life, but another part of me felt empty and lonely, even though I was always surrounded by people.

Life was hectic: I had to hold down a day job to pay bills, and then I spent every evening either in rehearsal or doing a show. One night as I was walking to the theater, it occurred to me that I could probably do a show every weekend for the rest of my life if I wanted to. For some reason, this notion terrified me. I quickly tried to think of something else.

But weird things like that kept happening. One morning while working at my office job, I found myself on the website of the archdiocese looking at the requirements for becoming a priest. I hadn't blacked out exactly, but I couldn't explain why I was researching what I was researching—I hadn't attended Mass for years, except for on Christmas and Easter. I didn't even believe in God—most of the time.

But there were those moments, late at night, when I'd catch myself thinking that maybe there was something to this God thing. Rick was no help in my quest to purge myself of any theistic or religious sensibilities; when it came to God, he was all over the place. Like me, he was raised Catholic, but he had subsequently dabbled in other Christian traditions. He even had a Bible, which looked like it had been read.

And then one Sunday night I came home from Vancouver, having spent the weekend with friends. It was actually a pretty big deal, the first time I'd flown on an airplane. Twenty-five years old and I had never flown. My mom was terrified of flying, so every family vacation had been two arduous weeks sharing the backseat of the car with my two sisters.

Still warm from my personal triumph, I noticed the answering machine's light flashing urgently. I checked the messages.

"Jake, it's Mom. Grandma's not doing well. I think you should come over to see her as soon as possible."

Grandma had been sick when I left on Thursday, but not that sick. I called my mother immediately, and she informed me that Grandma had slipped into a coma.

Grandma was now living with my aunt Maureen and uncle Jim, in a posh northern suburb. She had everything she could ask for, except for my grandpa, who had died nine years earlier. My grandma spent her days watching television; her shows were reruns of *Matlock* and *The Andy Griffith Show*, and it was no accident: Andy Griffith looked a lot like my grandfather.

When I entered Aunt Maureen's house, it was like entering another dimension. It was late, near midnight, and all the lights were off except for the television in my grandma's room. She lay there on her back, arms by her side, just as I remembered. I kneeled down next to the bed and watched the blue glow from the TV screen turn her incandescent.

I said a prayer or two, Hail Mary, for Mary, of course. I can't remember how long I knelt there or what I thought, but eventually I rose and lay down on the sofa in the adjoining room. Sometime early that morning, I was awakened by Aunt Maureen speaking to my mother. "Kathy, wake up," she whispered. "Mom is gone."

There was a wake. And at one point I approached Mom and Aunt Ginger and said, "You see, this is like any other family party—everybody's standing around mingling, and grandma's in the corner quietly judging everyone."

They laughed. They understood; we all understood. My grandma was an amazing woman with a sharp wit and an eye that didn't miss a thing. She was famous for her withering appraisals, including the time I brought my date over to meet her at one of my female cousin's weddings. Grandma was sitting in the corner, coolly scoping the room.

"Grandma, this is Katie."

"Nice to meet you, Katie," she said. "Are you enjoying the wedding?"

"Oh, yes, very much so. Everything's so beautiful, and the bride is gorgeous."

"She is," Grandma responded. "Too bad her bridesmaids look like the defensive line for the Green Bay Packers."

But after her wake, and after the funeral, something began to change in me.

It wasn't a burning-bush moment to be sure. It happened gradually. But, slowly and surely, what used to matter to me began to seem a lot less important.

I began asking myself what it was exactly that I wanted to accomplish with comedy, and more important, why? I knew I wanted to be on *Saturday Night Live*— that was the goal, that was always the goal. Yet it began to occur to me that once I achieved that goal, another goal would just grow in its place.

I realized that I always set happiness somewhere else. It was located with the *next* thing I achieved. If I get *this* audition, then I'll be happy. If *this* article gets published, then I'll be happy. Happiness was always at a different location from where I happened to be.

And then I found myself at Mass, by myself, by my own volition. And I found myself there the following Sunday. And suddenly I was going on Mondays, then Tuesdays. I bought the book *Catholicism for Dummies*, since I never had paid attention in CCD.

I bought a book on the Little Flower, Thérèse of Lisieux, my grandma's favorite saint and my mother's patroness. I read about her "little way," and it seemed like a far better way of operating than the way I had going. From the Little Flower I learned that the ordinary is extraordinary. I began to find happiness in the present, and all of a sudden, making people laugh wasn't the only thing; it was just one of many things.

I began to see a spiritual director, and I told him I was an atheist, and we talked about it. One day he said that he didn't think I was an atheist after all.

"Why do you say that?"

"Because you can't be angry at something you don't believe in."

"Touché!"

I began having long conversations with God, and I cried and yelled. I went on retreat, and then I went on another retreat.

I began to see Christ as my companion and friend, and not as someone out to get me. I was old enough to recognize that bad things happen to people all the time, but God is not the cause of it; God is the solution.

And then one day I was on stage doing an improv show, and in the middle of a scene, it occurred to me: *Maybe I've done all of this for different reasons than I thought.*

"I think I'm going to be a priest," I said after the show.

"I think I'm going to be a rabbi," Rick replied.

"No, I'm serious," I insisted.

"How are you going to have no sex?" It always goes right to sex in these conversations.

"The same way I'm having no sex now. But then it'll be intentional, not just because of my terrible social skills."

"You're a comedian!" Rick said. "You're supposed to go to Klown Kollege, not seminary."

"I think I have a calling."

"How does that work? I've never had a calling. I *want* a calling. I've tried all sorts of drugs and have never heard God call me once."

"It doesn't work like that. It's just a desire, a deep desire."

"What if you're wrong?"

"Then I'll just be a comedian. No harm, no foul." I pushed my cigarette out in the ashtray, got up, and headed out the door. Professor Paws whined at my feet as I gingerly moved through the door.

Rick called after me as I walked up the staircase, but I could barely hear it. Something . . . something about a disaster.

The Exorcist Who Saved My Life
without an Exorcism

Just go, you baby!" my cousin Denise hissed through her braces from the safe confines of Aunt Ginger's bedroom, where this, the most frightening and perhaps final journey of my nine years, was mapped out. It was a dare—a necessary dare—because I did not want to tell the truth about whether or not I still slept with a night-light. The dare hardly seemed proportionate to the truth not told, but I was not about to question the wisdom of Denise, who was four years older than I was and had a sharp set of nails she was not afraid of digging into my arm.

So I resigned myself to heading toward the indigo light that slithered out the half-open door of my grandparents' bedroom, where I was to watch five minutes, and no less, of the film *The Exorcist* playing on their old RCA. Denise would time this to the last second on her brand-new Strawberry Shortcake watch.

I peeked through the doorway. My grandparents lay on their backs, eyes closed, skin blue. I crept over to the vanity table and grabbed a hand mirror and tiptoed to the bed. I gently placed the mirror underneath my grandma's nose: the glass steamed gray. My grandfather's snorts were his giveaway. They were alive. My cousins had subjected me to numerous hazing rituals, which always involved sneaking into my grandparents' room late at night, so I was used to the mirror routine.

My grandparents usually fell asleep within five minutes of their heads hitting the pillows with the television still on at full blast. Both of them had an eerie propensity for sleeping on their backs with their arms at their sides, which, coupled with the glow of the television, gave them a supernatural incandescence that made them appear, if not dead, at least not of this earth.

What exactly was going to happen I did not know, but that made it all the more terrifying. This was *The Exorcist*, the mother of all scary movies. Forget your Jason and Freddy; they were mere pretenders. This movie was about the devil himself, the master of darkness, quite literally the root of all evil. Denise said that people had actually passed out at the movie theater while watching it. It was *that* scary.

As I moved from the tar-black darkness of the hallway, the luminous blue from the television caused me to squint as I looked into the room. Perhaps I could close my eyes and just pretend to watch? No. For one thing, Denise would quiz me on what I saw—she claimed to have seen the movie at a slumber party—and her nails looked primed for an arm gouge; and two, that would be lying, and lying was a sin. That was one thing I had picked up from CCD on Saturday mornings.

I flinched as I took my first look at the screen, my toes curled and the nails of my index fingers dug deep into my thumbs. What I saw was a huge letdown—no horns or pitchforks, no fire and gnashing of teeth, just a bunch of adults in bell-bottoms talking endlessly. This was the scariest movie ever? My shoulders dropped and my fingers relaxed. I bided my five minutes by picking at a hangnail and mouthing a song I'd just learned about the multiplication tables of four. I began looking around my grandparents' room to pass the time.

Craning my neck to get a look at the clock radio on their nightstand, I heard a crash. The grown-ups in bell-bottoms were really worked up about something, and then the camera cut to a little girl bouncing up and down on a bed, her eyes rolling back in her head, while a huge goiter grew out of her neck. She was saying the dirtiest words I had ever heard—the kind of words I practiced saying when the shower was running and I knew my parents couldn't hear me—and she was saying them in a voice not belonging to a little girl. This voice was raw, clotted and eggy; it sounded even worse than my uncle Bill, who smoked two packs a day, when he had bronchitis. This was the voice of something decidedly not human.

I shot down the hallway, leaped straight into my bed, and covered my head with a pillow, trying to smother the traces of "the voice" from my brain, although I could not muffle the sound of Denise cackling at me. *Let her laugh*, I thought, heart pounding in my ears and eyes clenched shut; I had gone face-to-face with the devil himself.

Fast-forward twenty years.

"Religious life? You mean like a monk?"

"There are other types of orders besides monastic orders," my pastor explained. "What about the Jesuits?" he said, as he noticeably slurped his soup.

"*The Exorcist* guys?"

"You do know that they have done other things, right?"

I was sure they had, but nothing could compare to being the religious order showcased in one of the most popular horror films of all time. I had even written my final paper on it for a film class in college—a masochistic move on my part because it meant watching the film, a five-minute glimpse of which had begotten a summer of sleepless nights back when I was nine.

I wound up watching it no fewer than twenty times, freeze-framing, fast-forwarding, and rewinding until I became desensitized to the gore and shock and was able to write a semi-academic analysis of the structure and content. What I discovered, once my fear subsided, was a well-crafted film that spoke to me spiritually at a time when I was not in any way spiritual.

Based on the novel by William Peter Blatty, the film tells the story of the twelve-year-old daughter of a film actress who becomes possessed by a demon while on location with her mother in the Georgetown area of Washington, D.C. After all medical and psychological explanations of the child's behavior are exhausted, the mother, a nonbeliever, turns to a young Jesuit priest-psychiatrist, Damien Karras, for assistance. Karras, along with his more experienced counterpart, Lankester Merrin, perform an exorcism on the girl that results in both their deaths.

What struck me most about the film was the character of Karras, a young priest, who, when we first encounter him, is struggling with what it costs to live the life of a vowed religious. He is alone and uncertain of his faith—a faith that informs every aspect of his life. His situation reaches an impasse when his elderly mother is institutionalized at a clap-trap state facility because he doesn't have the financial means to care for her.

My understanding of Catholicism on a cultural level, up to the time I saw *The Exorcist*, had been fairly simplistic, consisting primarily of Bing Crosby movies and *The Sound of Music*, films in which belief in God was both effortless and unceasing. *The Exorcist* was my first encounter with cinema that attempted to examine the complicated situation that is belief and the difficulties that can arise from trying to reconcile faith with experience.

Up until that time, I'd seen religion as one-dimensional, since it had always been represented to me as black and white; you either went to Mass on Sunday or you did not. There were no shades of gray, let alone blue, which I felt to be a more appropriate pigment for describing my relationship with God.

The way I saw it, God had taken away my father when I was six years old, and any and all attempts to explain why—such as "because your dad was so good that God wanted him to be close"—were insufficient. After all, God had a lot more good people to choose from than I did; perhaps God could take someone else's father—someone who no longer needed his father—because I still needed mine.

Watching this story of a man who had given everything to God only to have even more taken away and, who in spite of this, continued to do so—up to and including giving his own life—resonated deeply with me. There was something to this man Karras that I identified with—the pain he suffered, the confusion he felt, the questioning of his belief. Yet beyond it all was the deep-rooted faith that continued to drive him—a faith that could not be explained, a faith that surpassed words.

Nov. 15, 2003
4:57 p.m.
Subject: Come and See Weekend

Father Godleski,

Greetings and happy feast of the Little Flower. She is one of my favorite saints and I pray to her regularly.

Anyways, my name is Jake Martin and I would like to attend the upcoming Come and See Weekend at Loyola University. I am currently a comedian/writer/office clerk/waiter/receptionist/ telemarketer/dog walker/gardener—and also have a BA in theater and a minor in gender studies. I have not attended a Jesuit institution; however, I have had other exposure to the Jesuits and think that I might have a vocation based upon that experience.

Sincerely,
Jake Martin

Nov. 15, 2003
5:03 p.m.
Subject: Re: Come and See Weekend.

You can't attend the Come and See Weekend without my approval. I need to meet you first. When are you available?

"Btw" it's the feast of Teresa of Ávila, not the "Little Flower." Her name is *Thérèse* of Lisieux and her feast was two weeks ago.

Peace,
Dave Godleski, SJ

"Peace"? I felt "hostile" would have been a more appropriate closing line to the e-mail. The Come and See Weekend alluded to was a gathering for men interested in joining the Society of Jesus. The agenda for the event included various discussions on prayer; on the vows of poverty, chastity, and obedience; and on the history of the Jesuits.

As I perused the weekend's agenda on the official website, I was dismayed to note that none of the scheduled activities seemed to touch on the subject of exorcisms or demonic possession. I assumed this omission from the public record was meant as a deterrent to kooks and fanatics. Once the weekend got under way, the real candidates such as myself would be slowly indoctrinated into the inner workings of the Society and learn some of the various tricks of the trade, such as what really went on during an exorcism.

I thought maybe there would be an exorcism workshop of a sort, and while I did not expect to learn the whole rite in one weekend, perhaps they'd offer some tips for emergency situations, such as what to do when someone is possessed and no priests are available. Or perhaps they'd teach us how to identify those in need of an exorcism (I had a definite list of candidates from my job at the telemarketing call center) and show me how to whip the wand with the holy water around and yell, "The power of Christ compels you!"

If nothing else, I hoped there'd be a question-and-answer session with the top Jesuit exorcists, all flown in from places like Iraq and Georgetown (the two locations used in the film *The Exorcist*), who could answer my questions, such as "Is there any way to anticipate the projectile vomiting so as to get out of the way before it hits you in the face?" They would respond in hushed tones and indecipherable European accents while staring off into the distance at a demonic foe far too terrifying for the rabble to understand.

The abrupt tone of the reply from the vocation director, however, did little to stoke the flames of hope, and I began to think that using a film as my vocational model might not be the best blueprint for mapping out the rest of my life. The man who greeted me at the door appeared unassuming enough except for the shock of blond, pointy hair that stuck straight up all around the top of his head, making him look like a punk-rock Christmas elf. He shook my hand enthusiastically. "Hi, I'm Dave." This was hostile Dave? "Follow me," he said, and we walked to the dining room.

This was my first encounter with the Society of Jesus in the flesh. After our initial inauspicious e-mail exchange, Dave and I had decided to meet for dinner at the Jesuit residence at Loyola University on a chilly November night in Chicago. Dinner had already started, so Dave led me to the buffet. The dinner selection that night was fish or chicken. I was not particularly hungry, but I chose the fish because it seemed like the holier option.

Dave took me to a round table where six Jesuits sat, ranging in age from early twenties to late seventies. The youngest at the table, Joe, from St. Louis, introduced himself; he was in philosophy studies, the second phase of Jesuit formation. One of the older men was a math professor, and another guy, probably in his fifties, had just returned from Peru, where he had been working to establish an elementary school in an impoverished region.

"And what do you do, Jake?" The clanking of forks suddenly stopped and I felt the heat of their gazes on me; for once I could have done without being the center of attention. I focused intently on cutting my fish. "I'm a comedian," I mumbled—and involuntarily squeezed my eyes shut for fear of the reprisal.

"A comedian, no kidding?" A voice belonging to someone I could not make out through my squint laughed. "Do you know George Drance or Bill Cain or . . ." He presented a litany of Jesuits who were comedians, or performers, or who knew comedians, or who may have once told an amusing story at dinner fifteen years ago.

All of the men at my table were fascinated by the fact that I was a comedian. On the one hand, I felt as if I was eating dinner in a Petri dish; on the other hand, any concern about a lack of acceptance of my previous occupation completely flew out the window. I was inundated with questions about the life of a comedian: Where had I performed? Who did I know? Did I know that Bob Newhart and Bill Murray were both Jesuit alums?

After dinner, Dave took me to a small parlor for what he called "coffee and casual conversation," although it was not exactly casual, and I knew this would be an informal interview from which Dave would decide whether or not I could take the next step and attend the Come and See Weekend.

He asked me a lot of questions, mostly regarding my prayer life (I had one), my involvement with my parish (I was), and service work (I did). I thought things were going well, and then he asked me why I was interested in the Jesuits.

Did I tell him the truth? That my interest in the Jesuits was based entirely on a film that had been released twenty years before and was most famous for a twelve-year-old girl spitting pea soup on a priest? I wanted to lie; I wanted to tell him that I admired Jesuit spirituality, that I had read multiple books on the Jesuits, that I knew the life of St. Ignatius backward and forward, that I wanted to travel the world saving souls like Xavier and Ricci, or become a doctor of the Church like Bellarmine, or a martyr like Miguel Pro. But the reality was, the Jesuit I most admired was a fictional character from a horror movie.

Lying to a priest was probably not the best course of action in the discerning of a vocation. So I had to fess up. "Well, I really like movies, you see." Dave smiled patiently, but I could tell he was thinking that my love of film hardly made me unique among candidates for the Jesuits, or among human beings in general.

"And the thing is, when I was in college I took a film course, and we had to pick a movie to write our final paper on and I chose *The Exorcist*." Dave stared at me blankly, not making the connection I thought was so readily apparent.

"The priests in the film were Jesuits," I said.

"Uh-huh." Dave looked confused.

"And I was very impressed with the work that they did."

"In the movie?"

"Yeah, in the movie." If there was a way I could push my head down into my neck, I would have done it. This was not going the way I had hoped.

"We don't perform a lot of exorcisms, you know."

"Oh, I know!" I laughed, though my chest fell ever so slightly with disappointment.

"But, I do know one of the Jesuits in the film. Bill O'Malley, he was the one playing the piano at the dinner party."

"Oh, when she comes downstairs and pees on the floor," I said excitedly—and then immediately tried to bite the words back into my mouth. That was it; my vocation went up in a burst of flames.

"Yes." Dave laughed nervously. "That's the scene."

I walked out into the crisp night convinced that Dave thought I was insane. When I arrived home, I logged on and immediately Googled "Benedictine vocations," ready to take a new direction in the vocation discernment process.

An hour later, I started looking up some old comedy friends to see who could set me up with some shows to get me back in business. This whole vocation thing had been nice, but I was a comedian and not a priest.

I sent out a few e-mails asking whether anyone could use a spare on an improv troupe, or whether I could get in on a stand-up set somewhere. I wrote down some ideas for jokes and scenes, and then I laid down, told God that I had tried, and fell asleep in the holy darkness.

"Prayer before e-mail" was my mantra in the morning, but e-mail almost always won. The morning after my dinner with the Jesuits was no different. I opened up my account to see: "Re: Come and See Weekend." *Great*, I thought, slurping my coffee. *This must be the "Thanks for playin'! See ya, wouldn't wanna be ya!" e-mail that all the rejects get.* I clicked on the message.

> Jake,
>
> Had a great time getting to know you tonight. Your story is fascinating. Would love for you to attend the Come and See Weekend.
>
> Peace,
> Dave
>
> P.S. I love how you came to know the Jesuits, so original, I'll have to start handing out DVDs of *The Exorcist* with my vocation materials.

Celibacy in the City

I can always tell when a person's going to ask a question about chastity or the "sex-or-lack-thereof question," as I like to call it. These questions seem to be asked only by high school and college students. That's not exactly true, the sex question is pretty much the first question asked by everyone.

The minute I see the person, I can tell that it's coming. There's a hesitation and timidity to the raise of the hand that you don't see in the more strident hand raises of those who ask questions about my defense of Holy Mother Church. The interlocutor's head is usually slightly bowed, and the eyes are always directed anywhere but toward mine. There's a verbal shuffle of sorts, followed by some kind of giggle with a matching grin. Then comes the framing of the question within the context of "the vows," which always means *the vow*, but the questioner doesn't want to appear to be some sex-starved pervert, so he or she adds all sorts of window dressing about "the vows," all while I and everyone else in the room is wishing the person would get on with it and ask the sex question already. Finally, they ask, "How do you live without . . . well . . . you know?" When I'm kind of bored, I may respond with, "No, I don't know," but normally I take pity on the poor soul and answer the question.

The night before I entered the novitiate, I cried. I didn't cry because I was leaving my family. I didn't cry because I was giving up all my books, movies, and CDs. I didn't cry because I would be giving up dating, relationships, and all the good stuff that comes with those. I cried because I was leaving my cat.

Max was named after a character I wrote in a show I did upstairs at Second City. The show was titled *Cubicle Rats*, and, if I do say so myself, it was *The Office* before the *The Office*—a show about the intrigue, romance, and existential despair to be found in the world of the white collar. The *other* white collar. It was a full-length scripted show developed solely through improvisation. My character, the aforementioned Max, was a doer who never got a thing done, one of those people who always seemed to have a ton of projects in the works yet never had any output to show for it.

In my mid-twenties, I felt my biological clock ticking and thought it would be a good idea to have a child. Fortunately for all involved, I had no ovaries of my own and nobody willing to offer me theirs. So I did the next best thing: I got a turtle. The turtle and I had a symbiotic and heartfelt relationship, but sadly all things must come to an end, and on the sixth day in my care, my turtle, Terence, died.

Having shown no affinity for animal husbandry whatsoever, my immediate response to Terence's death, of course, was to get a dog. A few concerned souls pointed out to me that, given the difficulty I had with the upkeep of a turtle, perhaps the far more rigorous demands of canine care might be beyond my ken. I agreed wholeheartedly, recognizing that my full-time job, plus rehearsals every weeknight and performances on the weekends, left very little time for the kind of care a pet would need. So, naturally, I bought a cat.

I wanted a cat who talked. I mean literally talked, like those two Siamese cats in *Lady and the Tramp*, which I saw when I was a kid and had fallen in love with. Well, I didn't find any cats that spoke, at least not English, so instead I picked the one who whined the most. Max was a black cat I picked up at a shelter. Apparently, his original name was James, and his brother cat who had already been adopted was named Dean, but since I personally found the actor of that name to be over-rated, I changed his name.

My mother was concerned about the psychological con-sequences such a name change might have on Max, citing Charles Manson as an example of what could go wrong when a child's name is changed at a young age. I assured her that if I saw any warning signs of my cat starting a thrill-kill cult with him as a messiah figure, I'd be sure to change his name back.

I cared for Max much better than I did the turtle, and his constant talking became my favorite thing in the world. A problem arose, though, when I seriously began discerning a vocation to the priesthood and decided it would be best to move back in with my parents. Despite my mother's aforemen-tioned concern for Max's psychological well-being, my par-ents as a rule despised cats. I must say, therefore, they were good sports about allowing me to take Max with me, with the understanding that he was to stay in the basement. After an hour, that changed into the understanding that he must stay out of the family room. After another half hour or so, my stepfather might as well have signed the mortgage over: Max owned the place. (My parents not only disliked cats, but obviously they also knew nothing about them.) Within the span of a year, my parents went from committed, lifelong cat haters to bona fide owners of their very own kitty cat when I left Max with them and entered the Jesuit novitiate.

This was not an easy decision. I spent the night before I left sobbing through my Examen and petting my cat. I'd like to think that Max was representative of all I was leaving behind: a symbol of the sacrifices I was making, the loss of key relationships and intimacy and all that. In reality, though, my most meaningful relationship was with a cat.

The novitiate was located in Berkley, Michigan, a northern suburb of Detroit. The ride from Chicago to Berkley was about five hours, and I spent those five hours the same way I confronted all new and exciting prospects in my life: I slept in a fetal position in the backseat. Were I to have a name that truly defined my character and spoke of my essence, like a Native American name, such as Dances with Wolves, mine would be Sleeps in Backseat in Fetal Position.

Fourteen of us entered the novitiate that year. We ranged in age from twenty-two to forty-nine; some of us had multiple degrees and careers, and others were fresh out of college. Among us we had an attorney, a social worker, a civil engineer, and of course a comedian-writer-receptionist-waiter. We were all over the map theologically, with one guy referring to eucharistic adoration as "cracker worship" and another guy fasting on Wednesdays and Fridays and saying the rosary three times daily.

I was somewhere in the middle, both in terms of age and in terms of piety. I wasn't nearly as schooled as many of them were in theology, so I kept my mouth shut and observed and absorbed what was going on around me.

The novitiate staff consisted of our novice master, Bill; his assistant, Brian; Sister Theresa, who was in charge of placing us in our various ministerial assignments; and Walt Farrell, our senior father, who had a full-time position outside the community but also served as an exemplar for the novices. Walt was eighty-eight years old at the time and had held almost every significant position in the Society.

As you would hope of someone of his age and experience, Walt was, quite literally, holier than thou—if by "thou" you mean me, you, and pretty much everyone else on the planet. He didn't walk; he floated. He was like Yoda, but taller and with better skin tone.

Some of my fondest memories from the first year in the novitiate were of having breakfast with Walt. Several of us would gather in the dining room after Mass, and we'd ask him questions and hang on his every word. He was incredibly humble, patient, and surprisingly interested in our lives and what we were doing. He had no interest in comparing the present to the "golden days" of the past or in letting us know how things should be done. We would sit and listen, wondering to ourselves whether the legend was true and we were in fact sitting before the "beloved disciple" written about in the Gospel of John.

Memories of Walt are some of the few positive recollections I have of my first year in the Society—and by the time of my thirty-day retreat, I was ready to head out the door. I guess the transition is always difficult from the "real" world into religious life, but it can be especially difficult for those who have lived on their own and have had their own careers.

Autonomy can be a difficult thing to lose, and the sorts of images of religious life portrayed in movies—and let's face it, my whole life was pretty much informed by movies—were not particularly accurate. This for a number of reasons, but first and foremost because there are very few, if any, films made these days about religious life, and those that are usually come in the form of a documentary or in French, or both. American films on religious life are fairly nonexistent—outside those about demonic possession.

Again, most films about religious or clerical life were made not only before all the changes of the Second Vatican Council but also before the social and cultural upheaval of the late 1960s, which completely altered the face of film, moving from glossy Technicolor narratives to a rawer, authentic kind of filmmaking. Movies went from *The Sound of Music* to *Taxi Driver* in the span of a decade.

I didn't realize how deeply ingrained those movie-generated ideas of religious life can be, no matter how readily I could rationally identify them as illusory. When I entered the novitiate, I still expected something different. More specifically, I expected that the people would be different and that I would suddenly somehow be different, better, holy.

Of course, it doesn't work that way, and I quickly discovered that people in religious life are just as human as people in the regular world. Suddenly, when I read the Gospel texts, what began to stand out the most to me—something I had never really paid much heed to before—was what a pack of clowns the apostles were.

Yes, what a pack of vain, distracted, temperamental cowards Jesus had on his hands—and what a pack of vain, distracted, temperamental cowards my novice master had on his hands as well. Among the fourteen of us there were plenty of big ideas, bravado, and expertise—but for the most part, it all combined to make up a big pile of nothing. There's a reason they call it formation.

Formation is the time before priestly ordination. It was a rather abstract word to me when I first settled into my cramped room on Harvard Road in Berkley. Only during my thirty-day retreat in the novitiate, on the brink of departure, did I come to a deeper understanding of what it meant to be "formed."

There was a lot of work and a lot of travel; we were constantly on the go. The theory behind our constant movement was that our founder St. Ignatius viewed the world as our cloister. Unlike other religious orders, Jesuits do not take a vow of stability whereby they are bound to one community for life. On the contrary, Ignatius wanted us to be out in the world working with others. His understanding of the vows—poverty, chastity and obedience—was pragmatic. The vows were to assist us in our work, to allow us to be more available to the task at hand. This is not to say that Ignatius didn't find them edifying in their own right, but the work came first. Such was the emphasis placed on ministry that, at the time of their founding, the Jesuits became the only order to receive a papal dispensation exempting them from praying the Divine Office in community. It would be impractical for the Jesuits—working in a variety of situations—to have to leave their work several times a day to return to a central location for community prayers.

If the world was our cloister, then physical presence could no longer be the sole designator of community and companionship. This is why Ignatius was such a prolific letter writer. He saw beyond the boundaries of the literal and recognized that there were other ways to cultivate relationships outside face-to-face daily interaction. His letters were voluminous. As the first superior general of the Society he spent a significant amount of time writing to various superiors and colleagues while his "least Society" grew into something far larger than he ever could have imagined. His exchanges, such as those he wrote to Francis Xavier as he journeyed to the Far East and Peter Faber as he assisted with the Counter-Reformation in Trent, are testaments to the strength and nurturing that can be brought to a relationship through various modes of communication.

With the waning of vocations to the priesthood and religious life over the past thirty years, a strong concern has surfaced about producing more vocations. Historically, because of both the number of institutions and the number of Jesuits, vocation promotion had been relatively simple. Jesuits worked at schools and had positive interactions with students, some of whom would subsequently enter the Jesuits after they finished school; this was the pattern for decades.

As the number of vocations has diminished since the 1970s, the Society has been forced to get more creative with vocation promotion—that's where the novices come into play. Since the novices are new, fresh, and sprightly in their vocations, they're considered one of the best ways of "selling" vocations to young and youngish guys interested in the Jesuits. So my class, like the class before me and the class after me, was loaded into a van and brought on "vocation tour."

I liken my experience of vocation promotion to being in a boy band, or at least it's the closest I'll ever get to being in a boy band. I'd like to think I was the Justin Timberlake of the group, the superstar, the one they called "Father What-a-Waste," but in reality I was more like the Joey Fatone of the group. If you don't know who that is, then my point has been made. If you do, I suggest counseling.

I wasn't used to so much travel, let alone travel with thirteen other guys at close quarters nonstop. There were a lot of different, strong personalities in our group, and after about a week together we were no longer afraid to speak our minds to one another.

In her autobiography, Thérèse of Lisieux writes about the various idiosyncrasies of her fellow community members and the difficult time she had abiding them. She goes on at length at one point about one of the sisters clacking her rosary beads during prayer and how much it got under her skin. Clacking rosary beads? I wish! Try having to sit next to the same guy every morning at Mass who had breath that smelled like a combination of wet hay and scorched rubber. This happened every morning. I even offered him mints, but he said he didn't want to break the fast before receiving communion. "I'm sure God would understand," I pleaded through held breath and tearing eyes.

Then there was the guy who spent his free time up in the library learning Elvish—you know, the fictional language used in the *Lord of the Rings* series? You don't? Well neither did I until I saw my fellow novice clacking up a storm of odd-looking shapes on the blackboard in the library. Oh, and by the way, there's more than one Elvish language: there are hundreds of dialects. Yeah, I didn't care either. Still, every night my confrere sat in that library scribbling away with the intensity of Russell Crowe working on a proof in *A Beautiful Mind*, as if the fate of the world depended on his conjugation of the phrase *puntar aloymayar*.

There were of course the rabid social justice guys; there are always the social justice guys. Wonderful guys with fantastic ideals, and yet sadly it seems there is a strange correlation between the intensity of one's social justice convictions and the ferociousness of one's body odor.

And then there was me. The transition from comedy to religious life was rough. I spent four years of college and another five years in the world of comedy essentially being untrained in self-censorship. In the worlds of comedy and acting you must not be afraid of what others think of you or be concerned about what you say. To be successful as an actor or comedian, it's essential that you lower the level of self-censorship to allow for the freedom of discovery in the creative process. There are acting classes devoted entirely to knocking out the self-censor, to saying and doing the first thing that comes to mind. If you think that sounds ridiculous, you are not alone—so did my stepfather. And if you think it sounds childish, you are correct—that's the whole point. There's a reason it's called a "play" after all.

There's much to be said for being uninhibited and child-like, but it doesn't necessarily make for the best member of a religious order. Many times I cringed at what came out of my mouth, and many around me cringed as well.

When comedians get together, they spend the majority of their time throwing around bits. Bits of verbal wordplay that may or may not be used at a later time—often not. Throwing bits is the comic equivalent of a jam session with musicians. It's a great opportunity to try new things and to find the next level of humor in a joke. After doing it for more than five years, it became a sort of modus operandi for me, and I hadn't moved out of this mind-set when I entered the Jesuits. Subsequently, I spent a lot of my first year in the Society apologizing for things I said.

My first year of novitiate, in fact, seemed to contain a lot of apologizing. I prayed a lot, frustrated with myself and my inability to "get it." I wanted to be like the Jesuits I read about in the old hagiographies in the library. I spent a lot of time in the chapel, on my knees, begging for the grace to be more holy. I reveled in the fact that my primary work in the community was cleaning bathrooms; scrubbing toilets was very humbling and would read really well in my very own hagiography.

And yet there was always dinner—and always there I was with a one-liner. I just had to get in a comment. I tried so hard to be good, to act as I thought I should act. Sometimes days would go by wherein I would "behave" and say not a word. But temptation remained—always someone at the table would say something that just begged for a response, like a helium bal-loon floating in the air just waiting to be popped. Sometimes I resisted, digging my nails into my palms or quite literally biting my tongue to quell the impulse to say something. But usually I couldn't resist. I had to pop the balloon.

Often I got a laugh, but just as often my comments were met with silence. One of my fellow novices—a T. S. Eliot scholar, no less—once said to me, "You know, Jake, you don't have to say everything that comes into your head." Those were harsh words to hear, but they were true. I was like Whoopi Goldberg's character in *Sister Act*, except I wasn't on the run from the mob, I wasn't a woman, and I wasn't black. Other than that, it was practically the same story. I would leave dinner disheartened with myself and spent many an Examen frustrated and fighting with God, not understanding why he wouldn't . . . well, keep my mouth shut.

In the middle of my first year, my novice brothers and I headed to Gloucester, Massachusetts, which for those not familiar with it was the town where the events of the film *A Perfect Storm* took place and where much of the actual film was shot. The receptionist at the retreat house had photos of herself with Mark Wahlberg and George Clooney.

It was only appropriate that my thirty-day retreat take place on the site of *A Perfect Storm*; the irony was not lost on me as I set out on an experience that few people ever get the opportunity to do: to live and pray in complete silence for thirty days. It occurred to me how blessed I was, as I tried to imagine what most thirty-year-old men in the United States were doing during the month of January. Probably they were not sweeping the cafeteria of a retreat house, praying for five hours a day, going to daily Mass, and trying to avoid eye contact with everyone around them to avoid the temptation to laugh.

About ten days into the retreat, I sent my mom a postcard that said: THANK GOD I DIDN'T BECOME A MONK! Not surprisingly, silence and I didn't do too well together.

The thirty-day retreat is more properly known as the Spiritual Exercises of St. Ignatius, designed to occur over a period of four weeks, although the length of each "week" is not seven days but rather is based on the retreatant's interior disposition. The first week focuses on our existence as sinners immeasurably loved by God. The second week focuses on the life of Christ, and the retreatant meditates on various passages from Scripture, praying for a deeper knowledge and love for Christ. The third week is a meditation on the passion of Christ, and the fourth week focuses on the Resurrection.

The retreatant meets with his or her spiritual director daily for about half an hour, which is the only time he or she is allowed to speak during the day. The retreatant first discusses the preceding day's prayer periods, followed by feedback from the spiritual director and the assignment of new material to pray over.

I generally prayed for five hour-long periods and then journaled about the prayer. It was amazing to me how much time those five prayer periods would take up, and usually I was late trying to finish my last prayer period or two.

Our thirty-day retreat was done in conjunction with Jesuit novices from the East Coast, so there were around twenty-five guys at the retreat house along with a handful of laypeople who were also taking part in the Exercises. Because there were so many of us, we frequently had to share prayer space. You learn a lot about a person by praying in the same room with him or her, and I found myself developing relationships with people to whom I had never spoken.

Any retreat is special—the opportunity to deepen your relationship with God naturally begets loving generosity—but its effects are amplified just that much more within the context of a thirty-day retreat. For thirty days you and your fellow retreatants are on a warm and enveloping noiseless pilgrimage. My spiritual director likened it to walking into the ocean and delving beneath the waves into the serene stillness of the sea.

Being part of such a unique and sacred experience inevitably leads to a bond with your companions, whether or not you knew them before. When the retreat ended and silence was expelled, I spoke with many of the East Coast novices and laypeople, whom I had never met in my life, as if we were life-long friends.

During the first week of the Exercises I found myself standing on one of the enormous boulders that faced the rough January tide of the Atlantic. I was praying over the Gospel story of the visitation between Mary and Elizabeth, and somehow my runaway imagination took off. The rocks that covered the coastline inspired me and I saw myself—my six-year-old-self—being carried by Mary across the rocks away from the violent, ripping waves of the sea.

I didn't understand it for a moment. And then I realized that I had been carried through the time of my father's illness and death, not only by Mary or Elizabeth, who carried their babies, but through God's grace by a remarkable set of people who surrounded me. I had been carried to safety—and although there were moments of fear and tragedy, all along the way, through everything, I had been carried. I was OK.

I sat there, dumbfounded. Of course there were tears, but there was also the realization that it was *my* turn to carry, that now I must be part of the good for someone else. I realized that there had been people in my life who had affirmed and provided for me, who had let me know that in fact I was worth it. I was worthwhile, and now I was given the opportunity to be that person, that small voice of good for someone else.

This was no longer about trying to be a hero or a messiah. This was about being one of many—one of many for the good. I realized that of all the things I hadn't let go of from my previous life, the most troubling of all was my desire for fame. I wanted to be a saint, to be a hero, to be a Jesuit written about in books in the same way that I wanted to be on *Saturday Night Live*. So the problem really wasn't so much about who I was; it was about who I wanted to be.

Hebrew School Dropout

WWD? What would Walter do? Doesn't everyone ask themselves this question? The traditional format of this anagram usually involves the celebrated initials of our Lord and Savior, but the bar he set seemed way too high for me on a damp February night in Chinatown, so I chose instead to strive to emulate the most famous son of Shenandoah, Pennsylvania.

Trudging up the narrow stairwell of the four-story walk-up toward my first improv rehearsal in more than two years, it occurred to me that my boy Walter would've probably responded to my situation—that is, being completely bound up in fear and self-doubt—by praying. And so as I moved toward the end of a particularly dubious-looking hallway, I said the prayer that I often said before performing a show or meeting new people.

"Lord, please don't let me suck. And also, please don't let them hate me."

Sometimes I am a spiritual midget.

"How do you rehearse improv?" my good friend and fellow Jesuit Jimmy D. had asked not an hour before as we walked toward the Fordham Road stop on the subway. "I mean, isn't the point of improv that you make it up as you go along?"

Not exactly. Improv rehearsals are perhaps more akin to an athletic team's practice than a typical play rehearsal—except that instead of a bunch of sleek, well-trained athletes going through their paces with discipline and focus, the improv rehearsal primarily comprises a handful of fleshy, sallow-complected underachievers who spend the greater part of their "rehearsal" time gossiping and trading insults.

Unlike a play rehearsal, in an improv rehearsal there are no lines to go over, props to handle, or blocking to be set. Instead, the focus is primarily on drilling particular skills and techniques that all good improvisers should have at their disposal, such as agreement, heightening, and character work.

When improvising, it is always important to work with your partner to build and develop a scene. This is usually done by "agreeing" with your partner—that is, accepting and continuing to accept the reality he or she has established during the scene. An example of agreement would be if I were to start a scene by saying, "It sure looks like rain," and my scene partner were to respond, "Yes, it sure does." By agreeing with me that it looks rainy, my partner has helped to establish a particular reality about our scene, and the two of us can go from there. However, were my partner to respond, "It isn't rainy, the sun is shining," the reality of the scene is smashed and we are stuck arguing about the weather. There are few things less funny than two people arguing about the weather.

Agreement usually goes hand-in-hand with heightening. In fact, the two are commonly referred to in improv shorthand, as "yes and . . ." "Yes and . . ." simply means that not only am I going to agree with the statement you've given me, but I'm also going to add something to it to further develop the scene. An example of "yes and . . ." would be if my partner responded to me by saying, "Yes, it does look like rain, and I forgot my umbrella," so that not only are they agreeing with the reality I've established, but they're also building on it to help continue the scene.

Character work is just that: working to develop different comedic characters so as not to be stuck standing onstage talking as yourself, which can get really old, really quickly. Developing different postures, voices, and points of view are all ways in which you can develop different characters. Often these characters are inspired by people improvisers have encountered in real life. Most characters I've created lampoon someone from my circle of family and friends.

Another important reason for rehearsal is that it helps develop a sense of ensemble. The more often you perform with members of your group, the more comfortable you become, which leads to greater freedom and more risk taking, which lead to better scene work. At least this is what we hope. The reality is that improv rehearsal is a great excuse to hang out with your friends and goof off, all the while paying for a rehearsal space and a director to watch you. This is why improvisers are almost always poor.

As the rehearsal began, I relaxed a bit and began to feel better about my own, admittedly rusty skills. I liked to think of myself as making a comeback of sorts—although it was pointed out to me that famous people make comebacks, not people nobody has ever heard of. "Brett Favre makes a comeback," Jimmy D. told me. "You're just going to an improv rehearsal."

Going to an improv rehearsal didn't sound nearly as good as making a comeback, so I chose to go with my understanding (delusion) of the situation. I was making a comeback. I had finally made it to New York, and what better place to reassert my imposing talent than the home of the Great White Way? Yes, I do fantasize in cliché.

I took my first vows in the Society of Jesus on August 13, 2006, in Detroit. A week later I was on a plane headed for New York City. The irony wasn't lost on me that after all my years in show business struggling to make it to either coast, my much-anticipated arrival in New York would be as a vowed celibate and seminarian.

Perhaps more ironic was that I wouldn't be living in Manhattan or Brooklyn—the more affordable go-to location for most of my actor friends—or even Queens. Instead, I would reside in the Bronx. The Bronx: that most infamous of all urban addresses. Since the 1970s it had been emblematic of all things terrifying about the contemporary inner-city experience—crime, poverty, filth, and of course fire—who could forget the fires, and Howard Cosell's notorious cry, "There it is, ladies and gentlemen. The Bronx is burning!"

I landed there on a sweltering August afternoon at the corner of Fordham Road and Belmont Avenue, the screeching tires of the cab that had brought me from LaGuardia still echoing in my ears. There was a tattoo parlor behind me, a currency exchange in front of me, and liquor stores as far as the eye could see. I was smack dab in the middle of urban decay.

I would be studying philosophy for three years at Fordham University, the second phase of Jesuit formation, which consists of two years of master's level work in philosophy and one year of theology studies. I would be living in Ciszek Hall, two renovated tenements that served as hearth and home for approximately thirty Jesuit seminarians.

Ciszek Hall was named after Walter Ciszek, an American Jesuit who entered the Soviet Union at the cusp of World War II to work as a covert missionary. He was ultimately arrested and incarcerated at the infamous Lubyanka prison in Moscow, where he was placed in solitary confinement and interrogated and tortured for the better part of five years. Ultimately, he was sent to the gulag in Siberia, where he spent two decades doing forced labor, during which time he was allowed no contact with family, friends, or the Jesuits. After years without word from him, everyone assumed him to be dead. He was finally allowed to return to the United States in exchange for two Soviet agents in the early 1960s, and he went on to write two books about his experiences behind the Iron Curtain. Then he worked at the John XXIII Center at Fordham University until his death in 1984.

As a candidate for the Jesuits, I had read Ciszek's second book, *He Leadeth Me*, which focused on the spiritual component of his life while imprisoned and the deepening of his relationship with Christ in the midst of a desperate and seemingly hopeless situation. He was another Jesuit whose story of heroic courage fueled by the grace of God inspired my vocational fervor. Ciszek stared in the face of Red Army officers and KGB agents without blinking an eye, secure in his faith and buoyed by hope in the Resurrection. Those of us who lived in the residence that bore his name were reminded of our patron and his remarkable perseverance daily as we passed a collection of photos of him when entering the second-floor chapel for Mass.

But Ciszek's life of heroism seemed a million miles away as we plodded along, often begrudgingly, with our philosophy studies. Theology, we could understand, but why did we need to study philosophy? This world of concepts, ideas, and argument seemed so antithetical to the pragmatic way of life we had come to know as Jesuits. Where was the work? Where were the people? Where was Christ in all of this?

We were expected to work at a ministry of our choosing for a set number of hours per week, which was a welcome relief for most of us not keen on continually inhaling the rarefied fumes of academia. I worked at Cristo Rey high school in Harlem, teaching theater. It was while teaching that I began to realize not only how much I missed performing but also how helpful performing would be for me as an instructor.

So I dusted off my headshots, showing me three years younger and thirty pounds lighter. I began to audition. In the tradition of all great show-biz narratives, I got the first job I auditioned for. But, unlike the mythical tale, this one did not lead me to fame, prestige, or fortune; this was a standard improv gig. "Standard" means very little or no pay, an erratic performance schedule, and rehearsals at some of the strangest places and times you could imagine. Ninety-nine-point-nine percent of improv performers make little to no money, which means that they must work a day job. Most day jobs are the standard fare: waiting tables, clerical work, and so forth. I had done my time in most of them and had been equally deficient in each and every one, so now I was grateful that my day job was a philosophy grad student.

Taking the 6 train down to Chinatown, I was thrilled at the prospect of being able to perform after having been away two years. But exhilaration was quickly smothered by the rising awareness that I had forgot to mention one little thing to the rest of the members of my group: I wasn't Jewish.

The troupe I was working with was an all-Jewish ensemble called Hebrew School Dropouts. I would be the only goy in the group. During the audition I hadn't mentioned that I wasn't Jewish, let alone that I belonged to a Catholic religious order and was currently studying to become a priest.

In my defense, the audition notice didn't say anything about having to be Jewish. And I never told them that I *was* Jewish; I just never said that I *wasn't*. When you live in a community of thirty-plus guys, all of whom are studying to be priests or are priests already, and when you spend your days at a Catholic university, you begin to take some things for granted—for instance, that everyone knows you are Catholic.

And anyway, it was just an audition—what were the odds that I would actually get the job? An acting teacher once told me that for every fifty shows you audition for, you will get hired for one. Wouldn't you know it, my one hire in fifty came on the first try—which was awesome in the sense that it's always great to get hired, but it was also a bit disheartening when I realized that this means that I would have forty-nine consecutive unsuccessful auditions to look forward to.

And they were called Hebrew School Dropouts, not Hebrew School Valedictorians, so I assumed that my lack of knowledge of all things Jewish wouldn't be much of a hindrance. Still, I didn't know how to broach the subject with my fellow troupe members. It might not have needed mentioning at all if I had a normal life. But when you spend the better part of your waking hours serving Holy Mother Church, it becomes difficult to hide.

By the time I arrived at the rehearsal I had worked myself into a pile of knots. I have never been good at keeping secrets, although this stems more from a love of gossip than anything else, but I'm also pretty scrupulous about telling the truth (except when it comes to responding to the question, "How does this look?" from female friends; then all bets are off—"It looks great! You look awesome and so thin! You need to gain weight!"). By the time I made it to the door marked 3A, scenarios of me screeching, "I'm living a lie!" and them responding, "You are an affront to the Jewish people" were dancing in my head. Perspective isn't my strong suit.

During a break in rehearsal (there are always lots of breaks during improv rehearsals), the conversation inevitably turned to me, the new guy. "So are you single?" Michelle the unofficial leader of the group asked right off the bat.

What did she mean by that? In my paranoia I assumed that she was two questions away from a full-blown confrontation about the vow of chastity.

"Yeah, you could say that—my Facebook status is 'it's complicated,'" I said, in what I hoped was a hip, urban manner but was probably just a little bit confusing and a lot bit awkward.

"Oh, I know that one," Michelle responded. "One of those ambiguous 'are we dating, are we friends, are we just sleeping together?' situations. I get it."

No, actually she didn't. But I was too far gone, consumed by my paranoia over my own duplicity. The already-dinky studio apartment seemed to get smaller. What did she mean by "I get it?" What did she "get" exactly? That I was a fraud? An imposter? Was she about to expose me as the celibate seminarian that I was? I noticed my hands sweating, and I felt everyone's eyes X-raying me. I touched my neck automatically, unthinkingly checking to see whether I was wearing my Roman collar. I don't do pressure well, or as my mother likes to put it, "You wouldn't be my first choice for keeping classified government information."

"Did anyone see *The Office* last night?" Zoe asked the group.

"All right, all right! I'm a Jesuit! OK!" I howled, my head down and hands shaking. Walter Ciszek couldn't have handled it better.

There was a long and appropriately awkward pause. As usually happens in these situations (yes, sadly, emotional outbursts such as this one have been a recurring theme in my life), I quickly regained composure and perspective and begin to quite literally cringe at my own behavior.

"So, what's a Jesuit?" Mordy asked.

I gave them my story in all the gory details and I was met with a big old whoop-de-doo.

"We never said you had to be Jewish," Michelle said, matter-of-factly.

"I'm half Catholic," Kim piped up. "My mother is Jewish, and my dad is Catholic. Half Catholic, half Jewish. I'm a cashew."

Though I studied and lived in the Bronx, my spiritual life was stricly uptown, as they say, so it was only fitting that my spiritual director George Witt resided at St. Ignatius parish in Manhattan.

"So what's keeping you from performing?" George asked me, as I looked out onto Park Avenue during one of our monthly Tuesday visits.

Good question. The answer was always the same: fear.

"What are you afraid of?" George asked. It was our first session of spiritual direction, and George was getting filled in.

"Because I'm afraid of . . . the lack of reverence of it all, you know? The irreverence of it. I want to be a saint." I was all too earnest.

"Saints can't be funny?"

"No," I responded, still earnest. "Let's get real. At the end of the day, saints suffer, and the more suffering the better."

The whole reverence and irreverence thing had been something I had struggled with since entering the Jesuits. It was one thing to be a member of the laity and goof off, but even then, once I had decided to take the whole God thing seriously, I decided that it was necessary to curtail the funny—seriously.

I had taken my vows of poverty, chastity, and obedience. I had committed to a life devoted to serving Christ and his people. This was serious business. As a Jesuit I was now a professional religious and a "public face" for the church. I couldn't go around cracking wise and acting like a clown. God was serious business.

And yet I couldn't help myself. In the seemingly interminable solemnity of religious life, there were certain moments that just seemed to demand levity. Not during the consecration of the eucharist, mind you; but in the Jesuit world I inhabited, where everyone was quite literally offering up their "memory, understanding, and entire will" to God, taking yourself too seriously is an easy trap to fall into, and a little mirth every now and then seemed necessary.

The pattern that had been established in the novitiate continued. I would joke around at the dinner table, or in class, or at a community meeting. Most of my confreres would laugh, others would roll their eyes in disdain, and I would chastise myself for not taking things seriously enough.

We had two chapels at Ciszek Hall: the larger, main chapel on the second floor, where we celebrated daily Mass, and the smaller chapel on the first floor, which was no bigger than a large walk-in closet. I would kneel on the worn carpet in the cramped chapel with the sounds of the violence of the Bronx slipping through the windows and beg God to make me more holy.

Doing the Examen every night, I began to notice something interesting. Asking God to show me where I found him during the day, I noticed my thoughts returning to the television. Of course, the television.

30 Rock debuted the year I moved to New York, and I was excited to see it because some people I had known from Chicago were appearing on it. I wanted to watch it because there is always something exciting about seeing people you know on TV. I assume if you are really famous that thrill goes away, but for me it hasn't. I get a vicarious thrill out of seeing friends and acquaintances strutting their stuff, and because I worked during a sort of mini–golden era for comedy in

Chicago in the late 1990s and early 2000s, people I know pop up on TV all the time.

"There's my friend Mike!" I bellowed during an insurance commercial.

30 Rock, the story of the behind-the-scenes antics of the cast and crew of a television sketch comedy show not dissimilar to *Saturday Night Live*, was the brainchild of Tina Fey, *SNL*'s former head writer. Fey, an alumnus of the Second City, used numerous Second City alums as both regular characters and guest stars, and so the show became a great showcase for Chicago talent.

"That's my friend Jean!" I would howl as I felt the inaudible sigh of exasperation from my fellow community members.

"You're such a name-dropper," Nathan said.

"I am not a name-dropper!" I replied, indignant.

"Yes, you are. You just yelled out, 'Look it's my friend Jean!' That's name-dropping."

"That's not how name-dropping works. Nobody knows who Jean is. It would be name-dropping if I said, 'Look, there's my friend Paula Abdul!' Because everyone knows who Paula Abdul is. You can't drop a name that nobody knows."

"Wait. You're friends with Paula Abdul?"

Head meets palm.

I did my first show with the Hebrew School Dropouts at a small theater right off St. Mark's Place in the East Village. I wish I could say that it went well, but it didn't. It wasn't horrible, but it was pretty mediocre. I had forgotten about the downside of performance: bombing. That's when a show doesn't get many laughs and after a while you start to feel as if you're physically straining, so desperate are you to get a laugh.

It's an awful, awful feeling, and the worst part is that the harder you try, the worse it gets.

An audience can smell dishonesty from a mile away. When you start trying to force a laugh, to make something happen, any honesty that the joke or bit might have contained has vanished. An audience instinctively knows a dishonest performance. When you're up on stage trying to make something happen, and nothing is happening, an audience will not save you. They can't. They might pity you, they might smile for you, but they will not laugh. Not for long, at least. Laughter is too difficult to fake for any great length of time. So as a performer, when you're bombing, all you can do is try your best and try to make it as painless as possible.

I finished the show and met with my colleagues. When we had finished our postmortem, I headed for the door, ready for the long, lonely subway ride back to the Bronx. A bad show doesn't go away. The good shows seem to be fleeting; you forget them within the hour. The bad shows stay with you, sometimes for days, usually at least until the next show. You go over all the things you could have done differently; it's Monday-morning quarterbacking for the Saturday-night set.

Walking through the crowd, I noticed a familiar face. It was my Ciszek buddy Jimmy D. I ran over to him. He had never mentioned coming to watch me perform.

"Um, I assume you're usually funnier than this, right?" he asked immediately in his unmistakable Long Islandese.

"What are you doing here?"

"We all came down to see you; we thought it would be fun. What else do a bunch of celibates have to do on a Saturday night?" As he said this, four other guys from the community came over and congratulated me.

"Great job, Jake. You were hilarious," Chris said shaking my hand effusively.

"Thank you Chris, you are very kind and very dishonest. I appreciate that."

"I want wings!" Jimmy D crowed. "You want wings, Jake. Chris says there's an amazing wings place right up the street. But what would he know about wings? He's from Minnesota."

As we walked out into the cold February night, yelling and laughing at one another, a pack of celibates looking for wings in New York City, the show that had just passed floated from my mind like a balloon.

The Jesuit Guide to Very
Particular Minutiae

There comes a time when the perpetual job interview that is the life of the writer-comedian comes to an end. This occurs on one of two occasions: death or becoming Woody Allen. Otherwise, your life is essentially nothing more than a series of auditions, submissions, and meetings. When you are not doing those things, you are working, which includes inviting people to watch you perform who might be able to give you your next job. And they'll tell their friends, and so on and so on. So as you can see, the job interview never ends. And statistics show that you are lucky to get one job in fifty—and you know this, of course, so essentially the whole thing is one gigantic exercise in masochism.

I spent the better part of a decade on this hamster wheel, working on what I like to call "sharpening my rejection skills." And what most people don't realize is how much time, energy, emotion and, yes, money, go into the whole rigmarole. It's not as if you just show up at an audition from off the street. You need headshots, which require seeking out a competent photographer—because no matter how much your dandruff doesn't "read" in the snapshot from last year's Christmas card, that snapshot won't cut it with the folks at the William Morris Agency—and good photographers require money.

Then you need to make copies of said headshots, which cost more money. Then you need to send said headshots out to talent agents, hoping that your dynamic photo with your résumé attached to the back—revealing such earth-shattering information as your height (six feet tall with lifts, thank you very much), weight (155. Don't. Even. Say. It.), acting experience (portrayed Horace Beauregard in the Wilkins Junior High production of *Hello, Dolly!*), and "special skills" (languages spoken: French, Spanish, and Koine Greek).

And this is just the beginning. You need a gym membership to stay in shape, especially if you live in the Midwest, where running or using an elliptical machine outside is too much to ask in winter. And if you're not ridiculously fit, then the only other option is morbid obesity, which can also cost you a chunk of change (pardon the pun). Then you've got yourself some eyebrow waxing—for those caterpillars that appear to be walking across your forehead (this might be an issue only for myself and the guy who plays the older brother on *Everybody Loves Raymond*)—at $25 a pop, that can really add up. Then you need to get your teeth fixed, because even though you have a perfect bite, your teeth are too small and apparently hang from your gums like stalagmites (Or is it stalactites? I can never keep straight which one hangs down and which one grows up. Whatever).

And if you write, there is paper; or there used to be paper when you wrote—for sending out submissions so you can receive a form letter telling you how right your writing is for some other publication that is not the publication you submitted to because, "unfortunately at this time there is no place for your work in our journal." And then there is postage, and then there is software and upgrades and so on and on and on.

You could say that the business of being a comedian and writer is just that: a business. But then you would probably be lying, because in truth it's more like one of those scratch-off lottery cards my uncle Bill—the dark sheep of my mother's family (and by "dark sheep" I mean "male")—buys compulsively at the gas station for a dollar, except that instead of paying a dollar, you pay five thousand dollars and your odds of making a return on your investment are markedly lower than they are on the scratch-off card.

Then, of course, when you do get a writing gig you think, *I really could've just stayed in bed and watched my DVD collection of* Boy Meets World *for the past decade instead of spending all that time and money trying to make something happen with my "career" (yes, I do always put "career" as it relates to my comedy and writing in scare quotes—always), for all the good it did me.* And then one day, like Lana Turner at Schwab's, I'm sipping a cool beverage at a Jesuit residence in New York with my friend Gio and another Jesuit pal, when Jim Martin comes up and asks me to write an article for *America* magazine. (For those of you too young or not obsessed with film to know who Lana Turner is, she was kind of like the Lindsay Lohan of the World War II era, with a better work ethic and no nude pictorial.)

And yes, I did just compare *America*, a Catholic current events magazine, to MGM studios, and I do believe I might be the first person in history to do such a thing.

It was that simple—well, not quite. Jim did tell me that he heard I was a comedian. True. And that comedians usually had strong opinions about things. Truer. So he asked me to pitch an idea to him. Immediately, my out-of-work, desperate-comedian instinct kicked into high gear. I had seemingly never garnered a shred of integrity in my three years of living as a vowed religious. It was as if I'd never stopped auditioning—the grasping, clawing desperation, the sacramental character of any out-of-work writer-comedian, was out in full force. "*The Office* versus *30 Rock*" I spat out, and followed that with a barrage of ideas; they flew out of my mouth with all the subtlety of machine-gun fire. Jim gave me a look of what I think might have been subtle concern, but he continued anyway. "Why don't you just e-mail me your ideas," he said gently.

"Oh, right," I said, jerking my head back, trying too late to feign indifference and a semblance of dignity. "That's cool." I nodded and attempted to finesse away an errant strand of saliva hanging from my chin.

I decided to write a critique of Facebook, primarily because Facebook had become my entire life. I might be exaggerating, but not by a lot. I first heard of Facebook from my younger sister Amanda, who was in college. At the time, only college students had access to it, so when I started my philosophy studies at Fordham, I was excited that I would be a member of the select few (and by select few I mean one of the approximately twenty million college students in the United States) who had access to Facebook.

The moment I signed up was also, apparently, the moment Facebook became available to everyone. Like Groucho Marx, I don't have any interest in being a member of any club that accepts people like me as a member. I had already opened up a page on Facebook's danker, sleazier predecessor, MySpace, and had quickly become frustrated with the length of time it took to access any part of it. Also, I wasn't happy with the dubious nature of some of the content, and by "dubious" I mean I lost track of how many "friend" requests I received from "masseuses"; maybe I just looked really stressed out in my profile picture. I lost interest in MySpace pretty quickly and was disappointed to discover that Facebook seemed to be yet another variation on the same theme.

I wrote a scathing critique of Facebook, and I guess it went well enough because Jim asked me to come up with some more ideas for articles. As it happened, at about that time, I was falling in love.

Yes, this is where it gets juicy. This is where I get all *Thorn Birds* and write of bodice-ripping, forbidden love, secret meetings, and hours of hand-wringing agony as I was forced to choose between a life with God and my one true love. Just as Mary Tyler Moore as Sister Michelle in the film *Change of Habit* knelt at the front of the church, her eyes scanning back and forth between the crucifix on the altar and Elvis Presley singing "In the Ghetto" in the choir loft (clearly the spirit of Vatican II was still very fresh) as she made the heart-wrenching choice between Jesus and Elvis. Who could choose really? So, too, was I forced to choose.

Well, not really. I fell in love with a television show. *30 Rock* had entered my life and bewitched me, and I would never be the same. The creation of *SNL* alum Tina Fey, *30 Rock* focuses on the backstage antics of a late-night sketch comedy show. Costarring Alec Baldwin, Tracy Morgan, Jane Krakowski, and a crew of delightfully screwy supporting players (some I had known from my days in Chicago improv), the show managed to be both fast paced and edgy without ever losing its enormous heart. That's no mean feat.

My confreres and I became obsessed, not only watching the show in its regular runs but also later picking up the DVDs of the first two seasons and watching them repeatedly. Every night after dinner, six or seven of us would straggle into the downstairs TV room, which was about the size of a typical New York apartment bedroom—that is approximately the size of a contact lens—and watch an episode or two before going off to study or pray. The more diligent among us (or the more avoidance-prone, depending on how you want to look at it) stayed on and watched a couple more besides.

Structurally, the show is incredibly sophisticated, managing to weave multiple story lines together in subtle yet clever ways, with numerous callbacks and references to previous jokes and tertiary material all synthesized to create a cohesive piece that never feels contrived.

One of my favorite episodes involves the utterly catastrophic yet completely lovable Tracy Jordan's (as portrayed by the comic savant Tracy Morgan) attempt to win the affection of his sons by making the world's first adult video game. This is much to the consternation of his colleague and adult-video-game naysayer Frank (Judah Friedlander), which plays out via a narrative and cinematographic style directly pilfered from Milos Forman's classic film *Amadeus*.

This kind of referential, too-cool-for-school style has proved something of a double-edged sword for the show; it immediately became the critic's darling and swept the various awards venues, but the show's slick, sophisticated character proved off-putting to the American public. *30 Rock* has struggled and continues to struggle to garner a large following as the show flails about in ratings mediocrity.

The saddest part about *30 Rock* never attaining a strong following is that those who are turned off by the show's smug, hipster veneer are missing one of the gentlest, most big-hearted shows on television. Creating comedic characters is not difficult; it has been done before. The majority of all great comedic archetypes were created during the Renaissance, primarily by the commedia dell'arte troupes of Italy. And the majority of *30 Rock* characters could be found in a different incarnation on the streets of Naples five hundred years ago. What makes the characters of *30 Rock* unique is the tenderness with which they are handled both by the writers and the actors portraying them. Comedic characters are easy to bludgeon. They are created to be laughed at, and it is not atypical for them to be played and written broadly, one dimensionally, and cruelly.

A perfect example of this is the character of Michael Scott on the American version of *The Office*, as portrayed by Steve Carell. Michael is in the tradition of the high-status buffoon, the man with a lot of power and very little common sense. The character is written and performed in a one-dimensional condescending manner, which makes it very easy for the audience to laugh at him but also difficult to identify or empathize with as a person, because he is not a person.

By comparison, *30 Rock* has its very own high-status buffoon in the person of Jack Donaghy, played by Alec Baldwin. Yet whereas Carell's Scott buffoonery is alienating to his audience, Baldwin's Donaghy is a multifaceted, fully realized person at whom the audience can laugh but with whom the audience can identify. Donaghy is in believable, fully developed relationships with his colleagues—particularly Fey's Liz Lemon, with whom he has developed a paternal role much in the tradition of another show for the ages, *The Mary Tyler Moore Show* and the relationship between Lou Grant (Ed Asner) and Mary Richards (Mary Tyler Moore). And while Donaghy has his definite moments of buffoonery that fuel the show's humor, the "bit" is never at the expense of the character.

This is what makes a show like *30 Rock* special, transcendent. I would never claim that *The Office* wasn't funny, because it is; however, it lacks that thing that moves it beyond the ephemeral and moves television watching outside the realm of passive schadenfreude and into the realm of exchange and conversion.

"Conversion?" You ask, "By slipping on a banana peel?" Well, yes, in a way. Conversion isn't necessarily just altar calls and prodigal sons. Conversion can happen daily—and it does—in our own lives in small ways. It occurs in those moments that move us out of self for however long and that perhaps don't expressly move us toward God, per se, but at least toward the good—out of self and into relationship, generosity, and sacrifice. When a conversion occurs, our world gets a little larger and we get a little smaller.

The best comedy is rooted in honesty, in truth that is identifiable on a universal scale; it draws us in through recognition.

We laugh at the humanity of it all. There is nothing funny about perfection; however, there is much to laugh at with regard to human frailty. We watch a show like *30 Rock* and laugh as the characters attempt to control their own destinies, as they struggle to have it all and make it all work, as they try and fail to play God.

We see ourselves in these characters as we, too, scrap, toil, and claw to make the world work for us, and we watch time and again as it all explodes in our faces. When we watch Jack Donaghy attempt to maneuver and manipulate his way to the top of GE only to be inadvertently stymied by Kenneth the page, we see ourselves and our own selfish machinations and their ultimate futility. We laugh because we have been there: humbled by a God with other, better plans for us.

Drama is for gods; comedy is for human beings. Watching the finest comedy, we get a God's-eye view of how we relate to others and the world. A show like *All in the Family* put a mirror before us and our culture and forced us to look at our prejudices. We might not have been Archie Bunker, but the show made us look at those areas of life in which our own fears of change and desire for safety held us back. Perhaps we laughed at Archie Bunker in part because of our own feelings of superiority, but if we were being honest with ourselves, we were also able to identify our own prejudices and the limitations that they put on our relationships and our world.

The more honest we are able to be, the more mindful we are about why we are laughing and what we are laughing at, and the more transformative comedy is. Comedy doesn't happen in a vacuum; there is no such thing as something being funny for the sake of funny. We laugh at the guy slipping on the banana peel because he is human, and by definition that means that he is limited in his capacity to know what is going on around him. He would like to know everything that is going on around him and have total control, but he does not, and so he doesn't see the banana peel in front of him. The rest, as they say, is comedy gold.

But for every *30 Rock*, *The Mary Tyler Moore Show*, and *All in the Family*, there are twenty *Family Guys*. Why *Family Guy*? Because it is emblematic of all the worst things about comedy and why people of faith are so suspicious of popular humor.

Originally airing in 1999 and subsequently canceled two seasons later, *Family Guy* is unique in that it is one of the first television shows in history to be revived after a three-year hiatus, given its popularity in reruns and DVD sales. The animated series focuses on the adventures of the Griffith family of Quahog, Rhode Island, and various members of their community. The show is noted for its remarkably high reference level, but even more so for its downright nasty humor.

Topics for derision by the folks at *Family Guy* include Anne Frank, people with AIDS, and the mentally and physically disabled, to name a few. You know, the marginalized. Were the writers of *Family Guy* on the playground, they would be called good old-fashioned bullies.

Here's the thing. I have no issue with envelope-pushing humor—it's part and parcel of being in comedy. What I do take issue with is cruelty for the sake of cruelty. Defenders of *Family Guy* and its ilk claim that it is satire. Satire lays out a situation so exaggerated in its cruelty that it serves as a moral curative. Examples of satire include the film *Borat*, *The Colbert*

Report, and *Family Guy's* animated cousins *South Park* and *The Simpsons*.

Family Guy is primarily reliant on quick throwaway jokes and references; there is no trajectory or direction to the humor outside of the intent to get a laugh for the sake of a laugh. The humor neither is reflective nor has any movement. The show depends on one-offs and cutaways (when a scene quickly cuts to the future or the past for a brief moment before cutting back to the original scene) to play out their jokes, and these scenes don't really have anything to do with the larger-scale narrative of the episode.

By comparison, a show such as *South Park* builds a whole story around the particular topic it wants to satirize, making the intention direct and pointed. A one-off joke about Anne Frank says very little about the Holocaust, anti-Semitism, or anything other than the fact that it's a reference that everyone understands and that is universally regarded as taboo. To put forth a taboo because—and only because—it is a taboo is no different from a schoolboy swearing on the playground because he can.

It's no accident that my references continually return to the playground when referring to *Family Guy*. Satire requires a level of intelligence that the writers of the show have yet to demonstrate. The jokes are simplistic and mean-spirited and leave the audience feeling hollow.

In Ignatius's rules of discernment, he writes at length about the importance of the affective response in discerning what spirit is at work during prayer. I contend that measuring the affective response as Ignatius recommends, both during and after prayer, works just as well when watching television and film, particularly comedy. How do you feel while you are watching something? What kind of feelings does it bring up? Of course, laughter will be there, but we can laugh for different reasons. We laugh because we find something amusing. We laugh because we recognize something as true to our own lives. We laugh because we are uncomfortable.

What is it about a particular situation that we find funny? Why do we find certain things funny, and what does that say about us and what we value? We should be affectively aware not just during the experience but also afterward. What emotional residue is left after the experience itself is over? Do we feel energized and renewed? Calm and at peace? Questioning and thoughtful? Or do we feel angry? Empty? Guilty? Noticing our emotions can help us to better identify what spirit is at work.

Humor can be a remarkable spiritual tool, capable of healing, conversion, and catharsis. However, it can also be horribly malignant. Humor can hurt and can be damaging spiritually. A show like *Family Guy* does not feed your soul but rather steals from it. If humor at its finest is life giving, then humor at its most destructive can only be seen as life taking.

Prayer in 140 Characters or Fewer

When I was about ten years old, my stepfather bought me a video game. My stepfather is not a man of half measures. When he does something, he jumps in with both feet. For instance, when he decided it was time to settle down and start a family, it wasn't enough just to meet a nice gal, get married, and have kids, in that order. Instead, he chose to get married and have a seven-year-old son all in the course of one day.

I must say, I have always been impressed with my stepfather's courage, not only for taking on a full-blown family after thirty-some years of bachelorhood but also for marrying my mom and the four sisters and my grandmother, who came along with the marriage. It's strange for me to write of my stepfather as my stepfather because I've called him Dad for as long as I can remember, and he's acted as my dad for the better part of my life. But so as not to confuse you, dear reader, into thinking that I was witness to a resurrection, I will continue to refer to my stepfather as my stepfather. But I digress. I always digress.

My stepfather does not believe in half measures. This I can attest to after many attempts at mowing half of the front lawn and then being told to put down my glass of lemonade, turn off *Judge Judy*, and finish mowing the God-forsaken lawn. So I shouldn't have been surprised that my stepfather's idea of buying a video game for me was not an Atari 5200 console, nor was it ColecoVision, which included *Donkey Kong*, or even Intellivision. Nope, my stepfather brought home an actual, full-sized arcade video game.

It was enormous—my stepfather needed the assistance of his friend Pukee (yes, his name was Pukee, pronounced like the slang term for vomit with an affectionate long-*e* sound at the end, although I believe his Christian name was Lowell), who acquired the game via some shady dealings having to do with the game "falling off" the back of a truck. And it was an actual, real-life video arcade game, a tabletop version of the game. For those who don't remember tabletop games, they were just like regular arcade games except they were often found in bars, where the players could sit and play their game with the screen laid out flat on the top of a table, the easier to rest your beer and peanuts on while working to destroy the galaxy, jumping from lily pad to lily pad, or eating "pac-dots" while running from Inky, Blinky, Pinky, and Clyde.

My friends were duly impressed. "Whoa, this is just like the Pac-Man at Murphy's Law (the nearest tavern) that my dad goes to and plays when he and my mom are fighting," Jamie Bougher exclaimed. My friends' parents were a little less enthused. "Where did you get something like that?" Mrs.

Bougher asked unsteadily, as ten-year-old Jamie and I poured our heavily shaken root beer (to give it more of a foamy head, like real beer on tap) into pint glasses and water into shot glasses pretending we were at a real live shot-and-a-beer tavern.

"Don't worry about it," my stepfather replied, deadpan.

Computers and I grew up together; we were both in our infancy in the 1970s, went through puberty in the 1980s, grew into adulthood in the 1990s, and flourished in the 2000s. Like many siblings close in age, we did our best to avoid each other throughout most of our adolescence and ultimately came to terms with our mutual need for each other (all right, it wasn't particularly mutual) in adulthood.

I blame my indifference to computers on *The Jetsons*, the animated series from the 1960s that has played in reruns and will continue to play in reruns for infinity. *The Jetsons* were ostensibly a rip-off of another animated series, *The Flintstones*, which in turn was a rip-off, though two degrees away, of the landmark sitcom *The Honeymooners*. George Jetson bore very little resemblance to the great Jackie Gleason, either physically or in character. George Jetson was dull. Pretty much everything about *The Jetsons* was dull, actually, save for one thing: the Jetsons lived in the future.

The Jetsons was set in the 2060s, and it was exactly the future that I wanted. To live in a sophisticated apartment complex in the sky, to fly miniature spaceships to school, to push a button and have your meal prepared for you and a robot clean your house—this was the technology I was interested in.

What I got instead were endlessly dull lectures on BASIC programming in an overheated computer lab at Wilkins Junior High. Computer class in the 1980s was dull as dirt. There were no buttons to push, no robots to order around. There wasn't even any hacking into military silos and almost starting World War III (I was really into the movie *WarGames* at the time). Just dull, dry typing on a keyboard.

If *The Jetsons* were responsible for my distaste for computers, it was my own incompetence that ultimately drew us together. I waited tables all through college, and because it was the 1990s, of course, I waited tables at a coffeehouse. As I've already stated, I was not a good waiter. And when I say I was not a good waiter, I mean that there are people from 1998 still waiting for their nonfat cappuccinos. There are still busboys mopping up the tears I shed in the kitchen because I had three tables in section 4 seated at the same time. To this day I still have dreams about not being able to find the coffee pot to refill people's mugs. To everyone I ever served, I say that I am truly sorry. I'm sorry I rolled my eyes at your order. I'm sorry for mumbling under my breath when you asked for bread at your table. I'm sorry I spit in your—oh, forget that last one. Suffice it to say, I was a horrible, horrible waiter.

I didn't want to wait tables anymore, but like any struggling comic, I needed a day job. My friend Elaine worked as a headhunter, placing people in administrative positions at companies throughout the Chicago area. She suggested I try getting a job as a receptionist. "A receptionist? That's a girl's job," I said with disdain.

Elaine was nonplussed. "Jake this is the nineties, and the economy is so good that anyone can have any job they want. Employment is a buyer's market; Fortune 500 companies are hiring homeless people for their unique perspective. Art history majors are becoming CFOs; elderly women can be coal miners. Things like gender and what you studied in school no longer matter. This is the beginning of a remarkable new age that will never, ever end, ever. Ever."

So I became a receptionist. Because it was the 1990s, I worked for a "boutique" consulting firm, whose primary purpose, by the appearance of the staff, seemed to be keeping the folks at Ann Taylor and J. Crew in business. I learned that "boutique" is an elegant way of saying "small *and* pretentious." Apparently, there was some hip, wine-sipping, yoga-practicing, New Balance–wearing, upwardly mobile hipster cachet to having a male receptionist. It said, "Young, open-minded, think outside the box." Boy, did I teach them to never think outside the box again.

It was while working at said firm that I discovered the Internet; actually, I blame it on the woman I replaced. She wasn't leaving the company; instead, she was being promoted to consultant (remember it was the 1990s), and so she sat with me at the front desk for my first week, helping me to learn the ropes—picking up the phone and saying, "Good morning [or afternoon], Che Guevara Consulting. How may I direct your call?" (The company wasn't really called Che Guevara Consulting, but the IT guy, Stoney, wore a Che T-shirt on casual Fridays.)

In between the seven calls the company received between the hours of eight in the morning and five in the afternoon, my mentor, whom I'll call Bridget Jones—based not only on the affection she held for the fictional character but also on how much she perceived (read: wished) her life mirrored that of the popular heroine—taught me the wonders of the Internet. I had a lot of time on my hands at my job, and even when

I didn't have time (I often was asked to do filing or some clerical task), I made time on my hands (it's amazing how quickly filing can go when you don't, in fact, file but just shove everything in one drawer) and became a bona fide citizen of the World Wide Web.

Bridget introduced me to the remarkable world of message boards—online communities where people with mutual interests, such as movies and television, could share ideas and have thoughtful conversations about their shared affinities. Because message boards were anonymous, with members choosing their own pseudonyms, and as such, there were no consequences for any bad behavior—it became a free-for-all, complete with name-calling and tantrum throwing, the likes of which your local preschool has never seen.

In his brilliantly astute book *Snark*, which everyone reading this book should read, after reading this book, David Denby likened the Internet to the Wild West: There are no rules or boundaries. Each website is its own fiefdom, overlorded by a webmaster who is as kind or as despotic as the mood strikes. Rules vary from moment to moment; the Internet is the most thorough encapsulation of the pluralistic, postmodern world in which we live. Right and wrong vary from moment to moment and place to place. There is no accountability for behavior because everyone is hiding, freed from the restraints of good behavior and decorum by the enormity and remoteness of cyberspace.

This leads me to my confession: I am a troll. No, not that kind of troll. I am neither under a bridge nor do I have enormous pink fuzzy hair. For those of you unfamiliar with the term, a troll is at its zenith an Internet nightmare, someone who chases down individuals online with both technical sabotage and literary terrorism. I was a small-potatoes troll. Some might not call me a troll, but on the message boards that I haunted, that was what they called me, right before I was banned.

I lacked the technical proficiency to do any sort of real damage; however, I did use my literary skills to make some people's lives miserable. The Internet was like a candy store to me, and having never really developed emotionally beyond a third-grade level and wanting to "practice" my writing skills, I would verbally attack any and all who didn't agree with me. When I felt that was insufficient, I began to take on multiple identities online, creating new characters to antagonize community members with whom I was at odds.

Trolling became a daily routine for me, between answering phones and eating lunch. It was interesting to note that I still recall with great clarity the feelings of guilt and remorse I had at the end of most workdays. I usually went home feeling miserable, recognizing that I had wasted an entire day doing nothing but making fun of people for my own enjoyment.

I stopped trolling about the time I started going back to Mass. The fun I was having at other people's expense no longer seemed to interest me anymore, and it just seemed wasteful and unproductive. I began to notice at the end of my day how much better I felt after working all day. (Yes, I started filing, and eventually I was given more responsibility. Amazing how that works!)

One thing I didn't notice at the time but that has become clear to me as I've moved away from it is how isolated I became—not just within my online community but also with people in my life in general. I interacted less with the people I worked with, and when I did communicate with them, it was in the most superficial sense.

I'm still a big fan of the Internet, and I would be lying if I said I still don't think that I spend too much time online. It's easy to rationalize and justify being online, having to check e-mails, Facebook statuses, and tweets to see who's saying what to whom.

Like everything else with technology, the Internet can be a remarkable thing. It has made our world much smaller, which in many ways is a very good thing. Things like online bill paying, job and college applications, bank accounts, and e-mail have all saved us a great deal of time and energy. Even something as controversial as Facebook has numerous benefits, including reconnecting or maintaining relationships with those who might otherwise be long forgotten.

The Internet has the capacity to draw us closer together as well as to give us more time to deepen and foster relationships. But it is not a replacement for relationships, and too often that is exactly what it becomes.

I can witness to my own experience the ease with which cyberspace can appeal to the worst part of us. The scope and anonymity of the World Wide Web can be enticing to our sneakiest selves. It's the morally and spiritually disciplined soul who is able to navigate the Internet regularly without falling prey to temptation. As beneficial and resourceful as the Internet can be, there's a whole lot of wrong going on there and not a lot of policing going on.

This is where Denby's Wild West analogy is most compelling. Anyone at anytime can go online and enter a world of pornography, hate speech, eating-disorder propaganda, simulated sexual encounters, and real sexual encounters—and this is just the stuff I know about. This is the other side of the small world that the Internet has created. Because everything is at your fingertips—*everything*. The accessibility that the Internet allows opens portals for the vulnerable and lonely that they might not have discovered otherwise.

I have encountered many a spiritually robust soul who has spoken of difficulties with online content; pornography or sites about eating disorders seem to be particularly troublesome. These are people with full, rich prayer lives, dedicated to service and the sacraments, and yet they struggle. If the Internet is problematic for those living a life of piety, imagine what it's like for those without any spiritual rudder whatsoever.

In the Spiritual Exercises of St. Ignatius (founder of the Jesuits), one of the most significant prayers (OK, they're all significant, but this one always stands out) is the meditation on the Two Standards. A standard is one of those flag things that you see the knights carrying around at medieval dinner shows. You know the ones, where you eat a whole turkey leg with your bare hands while drinking a Fanta from a goblet, all while watching out-of-shape men in costume ride around on elderly horses and waving swords.

Ignatius in many ways transcended his time, but he never quite outgrew his love for all things militaristic. So it's no surprise that he wrote of the decision-making process in soldier's terms. In the world in which Ignatius lived, he described two camps: the camp of Christ and the camp of Lucifer, and the two camps are constantly in battle, waving their standards.

Ignatius's military analogy is a bit distasteful for some, when read from a post–World War II and Cold War perspective, but that doesn't make the truth behind the analogy any less relevant. The standard of Christ is to be found in prayer, sacrifice, and service to a life that transcends this world. The other standard emphasizes greed, pride, and power. It is important to note that these standards cannot be reduced to church and nonchurch; history has demonstrated the corruptibility and moral failings of the church, both institutionally and individually.

Perhaps this meditation seems a bit simplistic or redundant. Who doesn't know what the meritorious values of Christianity are and the life we should be striving for? And yet, I feel that it is the deliberateness of the meditation, the sheer pointedness of it that is important. Moral ambiguity is not something that came about in the postmodern era. Ethical muddiness is nothing new, and it was just as problematic in Ignatius's time as it is today.

When I began my studies in New York, one of the first things the community did was get together for a faith-sharing session, in which all twenty-seven of us told our stories of how we wound up at Ciszek Hall. When each of us had finished, we awaited the story of our rector, Vinnie (this was New York, so of course his name was Vinnie), a quiet, humble man with a wonderfully gentle Brooklyn accent (some say a gentle Brooklyn accent is not possible; I say they have not met Vinnie). Vinnie did not offer us a story but rather spoke of a film (my kind of guy). The film was *Moonstruck,* starring Cher and Nicolas Cage (if you haven't seen it, see it, right after you've finished reading my book). There is a scene in *Moonstruck* where the protagonist's mother, played by Olympia Dukakis in an Oscar-winning performance, meets a gentleman in a local restaurant, and by evening's end, he clearly wants to go back home with her. When she declines to invite him in, he assumes that people must be home and that that is why she turns him down. But she says, "You can't come in because I'm married, and I know who I am."

Vinnie said that was the best piece of advice he could give us: "Know who you are." We were Jesuit scholastics who had taken vows of poverty, chastity, and obedience, and for the first time we were leaving the rarefied and protected air of the novitiate and going out in the world to live as vowed religious. It was a powerful message for us, and ultimately, I think it is the prevailing message of the meditation on the Two Standards: know who you are.

The Two Standards is a startling reminder of the seductiveness of evil, which cannot always be discernible. Evil appears in many different forms, often under the guise of goodness, and it moves us farther away from God. Ignatius reminds us that, although much of the world appears to be made up of gray, instead of black and white, if we really examine and reflect on our own motives and the choices we have to make, we can discern which standard our choices fall under.

In his book about the Spiritual Exercises, Karl Rahner, SJ, one of the great theologians of the past century, if not of all time, in writing on the Two Standards maintained, "We have a tendency . . . to seek our own comfort, to make life easy for ourselves, to make no sacrifices, to make reservations" (Rahner, *The Spiritual Exercises* [New York: Herder and Herder, 1965],

171.) And it is from this fundamental impulse toward comfort and ease that we get into trouble.

The Internet then becomes a veritable hornet's nest of bad choices, impulsivity, and self-destructive behavior. It's remarkable how such an innocent-seeming activity like surfing the net can wreak so much havoc, but it does. Even leaving aside some of the more tangibly destructive aspects of the Internet, such as pornography and other such obviously sin-laden content, something even more pervasive and insidious is at work: snark.

Snark is not a new phenomena; it's been around probably as long as people first developed critical skills. However, as David Denby argues in his book *Snark*, the Internet has opened the door for snark to grow in epidemic proportions, much outside the realm of its usefulness (however small that may be). The Internet has allowed everyone to become stealth comedians, able to toss out mean-spirited one-liners left and right, anonymously and without any liability.

Snark isn't just limited to message boards and chat rooms and the world of the Web; its online inflation has infected the culture at large and taken over the realm of legitimate journalism. Snark has become a part of our cultural rhetoric, and what's problematic isn't necessarily so much that it's there, but that we don't recognize that it's there.

So what is snark exactly? I would say that snark is the comedic equivalent to kicking a puppy, and while we might contend that we would never laugh at someone who kicked a puppy, I would argue that if kicking puppies for laughs became the norm, we just might laugh or at least not call it out as cruelty. Snark is not corrective, redemptive, or cathartic—the most important attributes of a comedic type. Snark requires little thought and planning (which is why everyone can do it).

Snark is essentially the middle guy making fun of the little guy, which is counterintuitive to the structural form of comedy. The best comedy exposes the flaws and hypocrisy of the powerful. What Stephen Colbert (*The Colbert Report*) and Jon Stewart (*The Daily Show*) do on a nightly basis are both excellent examples of strong, thoughtful satire.

Snark is easy and fast, and just as there is very little preparation with snark, there is also no follow-through. The joke goes nowhere and as such becomes a mere exercise in viciousness. A recent outgrowth of snark that has developed online and in other forms is the assault on political correctness. This form of snark conveys that our culture has gone too far in trying to make up for the historical mistreatment of the marginalized.

People now put "politically correct" into sneering air quotes, discomfited by the challenge of having to alter their behavior and outlook for the sake of a minority group. It has subsequently become OK for comedians, writers, and denizens of the Internet to ostracize and stereotype the marginalized in the name of free speech and self-preservation. What this really is, though, is a resistance to conversion, an unwillingness to change our own behavior for the sake of others, for the preservation of our own ego and the maintenance of our position of power.

Snark feeds the worst part of ourselves, and I can attest to its power. I have certainly fallen victim to its appeal on many occasions, and I still do. It is a dangerous instrument, primarily because it seems so harmless—after all, what's one little dig here or there?—but it has led to a cultural mind-set that is unhealthy and becomes more and more difficult to discern the more embedded it becomes. Suddenly, the Two Standards aren't quite so easy to differentiate as we thought.

Guest Lecturer at Klown Kollege

Here are some atheists you should know," I began. Immediately, all eyes in front of me rolled heavenward. This wasn't how it was supposed to happen. There were supposed to be grunts of interest and exclamations of intrigue, hands waving madly in the air as the students yelled over one another, passionately declaring their views, faces burning red with intensity. They would care, and they would be invested; freshman religion would change their lives. And it would all be because of me—Jake Martin: messiah and miracle worker.

For the preceding twelve weeks I had tossed out one theological topic after another, hoping that something, anything, would pique the curiosity of my crew of unchurched, indifferent, and decidedly secular fourteen-year-olds. Helplessly, I stood at the front of the classroom, talking on subjects ranging from the early Christians in Rome to the seven sacraments—all of which were met with the same wall of faces bowed in contempt.

I could understand their disinterest to a point. What does the creed, be it Nicene or Apostle's, have to do with the world of an American teenager brought up in a culture lacking in absolutes? A concept such as Trinitarian theology—even with my oh-so-clever demonstration using an Oreo cookie (three parts, one cookie, get it?)—meant nothing to their tweeting and texting world.

But with atheism, I thought I had them. I mean, come on! This was atheism! It was current, it was hip, and everyone was doing it! For the love of God, it was *them*! They were atheists! They didn't believe! That's why they rolled their eyes at all this stuff in the first place!

This, I thought, would be my chance to be *that* Jesuit. You know the one? *That* Jesuit, who pushes boundaries and shakes the status quo; the one with his finger on the pulse of the youth of America; the one who was going to awaken an apathetic, lethargic generation from its malaise and bring forth a thriving, vibrant church for the new millennium. I was going to be *that* Jesuit.

I would be a nonsecular Robin Williams in *Dead Poets Society*, standing on desks and bellowing overused Latin platitudes to my young minions as they drank up each cliché I spewed as if it were mother's milk. I would be Robert Donat in *Goodbye, Mr. Chips*, without the dead wife. I would be Sydney Poitier in *To Sir, with Love*, except I wouldn't be in England or black. I would be Edward James Olmos in *Stand and Deliver*, except instead of teaching an at-risk Latino population in Los Angeles I would be teaching an affluent, upper-middle-class, predominantly white suburban community on Chicago's North Shore.

I would be, as my friend Joanna said when I told her I was entering the Jesuits, "the cool priest who wears high-tops underneath his cassock and shoots hoops with the kids on the playground." I would make a difference in their lives! I would save them! From what, I didn't know exactly: a semi-secular culture, consumerism, or the devil himself perhaps. Whatever it was didn't matter nearly as much as the fact that I, Jake Martin—messiah and miracle worker—would save them, damn it, whether they liked it or not!

There's a thin line between altruism and a messiah complex, and I suspect at one point or another many of us cross it. I have found that most Jesuits tend to live their lives on the border between the two, which is why it's so important that we have non-Jesuits in our lives to continually remind us to get over ourselves. It's also why at some point in our formation all of us are required to teach high school; nothing will let you know quicker than a room full of fourteen-year-olds that you are completely and utterly dependent on God for everything.

Atheism wasn't happening for my freshmen. Those who managed to stay awake stared blankly—bovinely, if you will—slow, compliant, and utterly disinterested. Except one. Joey Hagen, whose smile was hidden somewhere beneath a vast assemblage of twisting wire and steel brackets. Alas, I knew that the gleam in his eyes had nothing to do with any sort of enthusiasm for the topic at hand and everything to do with my recent disclosure of our shared love for steak burritos from the fast-food franchise Chipotle.

I trudged through my lesson, disheartened but determined. "Here are the three atheists you should know and why," I said. "I don't expect most of you to be familiar with the first two, but you've probably heard of the third. The first two are Karl Marx and Friedrich Nietzsche, and the third is Sigmund Freud. Now, who knows who Sigmund Freud is?"

I was delighted to see an array of hands shoot up and surprised to see Joey among them, as he usually raised his hand only to ask questions related to my preferences in fast food; the cast members I knew from *Saturday Night Live*; and, of course, the inevitable, "As a Jesuit is it true that you can't have sex or that you can but just can't get married?"

"Joe, now remember, no more Chipotle. This is about Sigmund Freud, right?"

He grinned his wire grin and shook his head with certitude. "No, I know this," he said with the assurance of Alex Trebek. "He was a lion tamer."

The look of bafflement on my face was matched by the look of hope and earnestness spread across his. Sigmund Freud, lion tamer? *Lion tamer?* I had no response other than the obvious and emphatic no. But I just couldn't do that. Joe was a sweet, smart kid who lacked self-confidence, and I didn't have the heart to tell him that he was wrong. I also had absolutely no idea what he was talking about or where his idea that Sigmund Freud was a circus performer came from. So, instead of responding right away, I did what I normally do in a crisis: nothing. I stared at him, frozen, with a smile of confusion plastered across my face. Joe beamed right back at me. We stayed like that, staring and smiling, for what seemed like a long time, an uncomfortably long time.

Had it been up to me, we would have stayed in that awkward, silent stalemate until the bell rang for the end of class twenty minutes later. Fortunately, cooler heads prevailed, and Eloise, one of my brighter charges, piped up: "You mean Siegfried and Roy! Not Sigmund Freud! " Mercifully, she had no concern for shattering Joe's self-esteem for the sake of factual accuracy.

Ah, yes, Siegfried and Roy! It all made sense. I exhaled deeply. Then I caught myself: *Now it makes sense?*

"Klown Kollege" was a phrase I coined for any group of students who were chattering, giggling, or passing notes while I was talking in class. Like a good comedian, I had stolen the line from someone else (in this case, Tina Fey) and used it for my own end, which had nothing to do with a slot on Letterman. I used "Klown Kollege" primarily to firmly but gently regain focus during class.

I was in the regency phase of my Jesuit formation, which occurs between philosophy and theology studies. It is the opportunity for a young Jesuit to work and live full-time in an apostolate—a specific Jesuit ministry. I was assigned to Loyola Academy in Wilmette, Illinois, approximately forty minutes from where I grew up geographically and approximately 150 million light years away culturally.

Loyola—or LA, as it's called to those in the know, which can be confusing and disappointing for an actor such as myself, who, when first told I was going to LA, had visions of palm trees and Julia Roberts dancing in my head—is the largest Jesuit secondary school in the United States. It is a co-ed school located right smack dab in the middle of Chicago's affluent North Shore.

There is a fair bit of controversy among Jesuits these days about our work in what are called our *traditional* institutions, that is, those institutions that have been around a century or so and primarily serve a fairly moneyed population. This is in contrast to our newer works, which deal primarily with lower socioeconomic communities, such as the original Cristo Rey High School in Chicago's Pilsen neighborhood, located about half an hour south of Loyola Academy.

I have often been asked by my fellow Jesuits why I chose to work at a more traditional apostolate over a newer work, as many of my confreres did. (This question is never innocent; there is always an agenda behind it.) Ultimately, however, my choice came down to the fact that I didn't know how to teach. I had taught improv and acting classes on and off for years, but real, actual, full-time, five-days-a-week, five-sections-a-day classroom teaching was not something with which I was at all familiar.

Having come from a family of teachers, I had enough respect for the profession to proceed with caution into my initial foray into the classroom. I figured I would be of no use to anyone heading into one of our newer works, where the infrastructures were still being developed and I would be learning to teach on the fly. It made more sense to me to work in a well-oiled machine like Loyola, which offered the resources I needed to help me cultivate the good teaching skills.

During my first semester at Loyola, I was given a mentor teacher whom I would be observing for the first few weeks, before taking on a unit of my own. It was decided that I would teach both theater and theology: one section of theater in the morning and two of theology in the afternoon. Things went remarkably well, and by the end of the semester I was ready to teach on my own full-time.

Teaching proved to be simultaneously a life-giving, all-enveloping encounter with God's love and the most abhorrent, blood-curdling, soul-destroying experience of my life. That's teaching—or at least that's the first year of teaching. It reached its nadir while I was proctoring a standardized test. Proctoring, which is a sophisticated word for "babysitting," is always horrific because you're usually not with your own students but rather with a pack of strangers who would like nothing better than to upend your mental health for their own personal enjoyment.

For my first proctoring experience I was in charge of a group of sophomores who took it upon themselves to make my life a living hell. How, you may ask, could a group of fifteen-year-olds do such a thing? Why, very easily, almost as if they were born solely for that purpose: repeatedly asking me to reread instructions, spell words they already knew, and for all intents and purposes make me look like an idiot—not a difficult task even in the best of circumstances.

As we came to the end of the three-and-a-half-hour ordeal and embarked on the final portion of the exam, I again encountered another barrage of inane questions and requests. Finally, when one of the boys, yet again, asked, "Where do I put my name?"—which was, yet again, met with a round of unsuccessfully stifled laughs—I heard myself respond, "What are you, a moron?" I said another word, too, an adjective—well, at least this time it was an adjective.

I gasped the minute I said it, and it echoed the gasp that came from the twenty-some fifteen-year-olds sitting before me. I apologized immediately, and then I apologized again, and again. I was going to be fired. Great. I would be the first

Jesuit in history fired for dropping the *F* bomb in the class-room. Surely, there was nothing written about this in the *Ratio Studiorum,* the official design for Jesuit education, writ-ten in 1599.

As it turned out, I was just reprimanded, but I was shaken. I saw I was going to need to step it up in the God department if I were to survive three years of teaching.

My prayer time had slackened a bit in the carefree days of philosophy studies because the lifestyle of a young Jesuit dur-ing this time is pretty laid back, and it can be easy to pick up bad habits. As a former drinker and smoker, I can attest to the fact that my ability to pick up bad habits is, though not Charlie Sheenesque in scale, certainly right up there. Work-ing with teenagers full-time, however, meant that I needed to pray just as much as I needed to eat (which I was doing a lot of—especially at night, and especially cookies), sleep (which I wasn't doing enough of—especially at night, hence the cook-ies), and breathe (which I was doing most of the time—while eating cookies).

Prayer in the morning and before bed became essential. I needed to be speaking to God and, more important, listening to God—especially before I spoke or listened to anyone else. Just as important, if not more so, I needed to be reflecting on the events of the day just passed. Ignatius said that if you give up every other aspect of prayer, whatever you do, do not give up praying the Examen.

The Examen was the perfect way to identify the areas in which I fell short. I could begin to identify patterns in my behavior that were problematic and bring them to prayer and spiritual direction. The Examen wound up altering my perspective significantly. There is nothing like a thorough, honest daily Examen to hike up your humility levels; sitting before your loving creator, fully open and vulnerable, acknowledging your sinfulness and asking for help is the perfect recipe for recognizing your own powerlessness. The lesson is repeated over and over: I am not God, nor should I attempt to be.

Through the Examen I was also able not only to identify what was going on with me but also to have a better understanding of what was going on with my students. I began to think about the conversations we had in class, which more often than not devolved into conversations about TV and movies. Mind you, this wasn't necessarily a part of my lesson plan, but as my students learned fairly quickly, I am easily distracted, especially when it comes to TV and film.

The speed with which I can fly off topic amazes me at times. I will be leading a discussion about the Edict of Milan, and before I know it, I'm talking about Snooki on *Jersey Shore*! (To be fair, it was the fourth season of the show, and Snooki and friends were living in Italy.) Like any self-respecting high school students worth their weight in forty-ounce cans of energy drinks, the moment they discover my "idiosyncrasy" (as I like to call it), they run with it and never look back.

"Mr. Martin, who's your favorite character in *Anchor Man*?"

"Not now, Sean. You're not going to get me this time. We're talking about Original Sin. . . . But I think it would be Ron, or maybe Brick. 'I love lamp.' God, I love that movie."

Some of my more intelligent students are savvy enough to massage the topic at hand into a pop-culture detour.

"And so Ignatius experienced his first conversion," I lectured, as pious as Pope Pius I, noticing Kathleen beaming and waving her hand in the air. "Uh . . . yes, Kathleen?"

"So Ignatius was kind of like Serena from *Gossip Girl*, because she left New York and came back and wanted to change her ways after sleeping with Blair's boyfriend."

"Sort of, Kathleen, except Serena hasn't really changed her ways all that much . . ." Well, you get the idea.

No one is more influenced, swayed, and vulnerable to the ebb and flow of the waves of popular culture than teenagers, especially high school freshmen. Why freshmen, in particular? Freshman year is a time of transition, and with it comes full indoctrination into the world of teenage culture. A freshman's social identity within the high school world is not clearly defined, and to many freshman, if not most, the physical changes they are undergoing go a long way toward defining their identity and self-perception. A star athlete in eighth grade, for instance, might not grow enough to continue being a star athlete in high school, and so subsequently has to find new ways of finding affirmation and esteem.

Add to that the multiple social dimensions that the freshman encounters for the first time. Relationships move beyond the familial and the parochial. For the first time, a significant portion of the teenager's time is spent away from the family and is instead spent with peers. This new social paradigm includes a new set of social regulations. What develops is a community of embryonic souls in desperate need of guidance and direction—souls who are simultaneously at a stage of development that is fundamentally resistant to any explicit form of guidance and direction. Enter television, film, and popular culture.

What's so appealing to teenagers (and, in a more limited sense, to all of us) about popular culture, particularly television and film, is that it serves as an instruction manual for living without appearing to do so. It illustrates in an unassuming manner what is correct behavior and what is not, and it does so in a way that is neither didactic nor preachy. In other words, it doesn't tell; it shows.

Television and film demonstrate an ideal, and while most teenagers will tell you that they know that what they're watching is fantasy, very few of them would or could claim that a significant part of themselves has not been invested in the ideal that fantasy puts forth. While the goals are different, the means are similar to Aristotelian ethics, wherein a standard is established to which one continually aims, all the time recognizing that one will inevitably fall short.

The cultural impact of a show such as *Jersey Shore* can be found most readily among its teenage audience. Indeed, I first learned of the show from my students, all of whom seemed to be obsessed with the hijinks of this band of cartoonish twentysomethings.

The cartoonish quality is what almost salvages the show; what works for this "reality" show is, in fact, its unreality. It is the grotesquerie of the cast's appearance and behavior—the sheer inconceivability that these people could possibly be authentic or that what is occurring in their life is in any way steeped in reality—that almost redeems the show. An adult viewer can watch *Jersey Shore* and compartmentalize it, recognizing it for what it is: an absurdist trifle, a pseudovoyeuristic exercise in the dangers of a consumerist, appearance-obsessed culture.

The primary audience for the show, however, is teenagers, who, while perhaps able to recognize the absurdity of the participants and their various machinations, are unable to recognize the underlying emptiness at the show's core. They laugh at the absurdity of the situations in which the protagonists find themselves, but at the same time they fail to recognize the fundamental lack of values that drives every aspect of the show. They see physical violence—the standard culmination of each episode—as conflict resolution, anonymous sex as intimacy, and binge drinking as a panacea, all while never recognizing that amid all the chaos, absolutely nothing of substance is occurring.

The show is really a study of that aspect of American culture that has mistaken chaos and disorder for meaning and relevance. Each week millions tune in to watch this group of overly tanned, overly gelled, overly sexed twentysomethings attempt to drink, fight, and couple their way into some sort of an identity. This then becomes the model for living for the teenager, a series of actions—sex, violence, and substance abuse—void of any content. *Jersey Shore* is not alone in this regard; it's just the most conspicuous example.

I begin each of my freshman theology classes with what I call an "opener." It's a pretty standard pedagogical device used to focus students' attention at the beginning of class. I write out a question on the board related to the particular subject of that day's lesson. The students, upon entering the classroom, write down their responses in a notebook, and later we discuss their responses—and I relate them back to what I am teaching that day.

A recent opener was on the term *sacrament*. To introduce the subject, I offered this opener: "Have you ever had an experience of awe and wonderment?" I hoped to receive responses about experiences related to the natural world—a sunset or a starry night—a common entry into the world of Ignatian spirituality.

After we said our opening prayer, I went around the class and asked the students for their responses. For the most part they were exactly what I wanted to hear: views from mountaintops, pristine lakes, the Grand Canyon. Of course, because they were high school freshmen, there was also the occasional cheeseburger from Five Guys, making it onto the football team, and seeing Megan Fox in the *Transformers* movie for the first time.

And then Jack responded: "There are a lot of stereotypes about priests and stuff, and you usually think of them being a certain way, like really holy and strict. But then I met you and you're totally not like that. You're cool."

I write this not because I want to show how cool and great I am (but seriously, I am) but because it reminded me that it can be pretty easy to bemoan all that is wrong with youth culture—and shows like *Jersey Shore* don't help the matter. But to paraphrase St. Ignatius, it is our duty as evangelizers to "enter through their door," and sometimes that door can be pretty gross.

Gross-out humor has been around since teenage boys learned that they could make repulsive noises with their armpits. In recent years, however, it has moved out of the high school locker room and into the mainstream. It's difficult to pinpoint when this transition in popular culture occurred, but my own opinion is that the success of the film *There's Something about Mary* in 1998 was when it really took off.

There's Something about Mary was written, produced, and directed by Peter and Bobby Farrelly, who seemed to have cornered the market on the gross-out genre. Most people expected that with the waning of their success following *Mary*, gross-out comedy would wane as well. But it didn't. In fact, gross-out comedy just got bigger, thanks in no small part to a collection of actors and writers previously known for a critically acclaimed but quickly canceled television series from the late 1990s about, what else, high school: *Freaks and Geeks*. At the helm of this small coterie of talented individuals was the creator and producer of *Freaks and Geeks*, Judd Apatow.

In the summer of 2004, Apatow produced *Anchorman: The Legend of Ron Burgundy*, starring *Saturday Night Live* alum Will Ferrell, which exceeded all expectations and became both a critical and a box-office phenomenon. The film's mix of gross-out, referential, and absurdist humor hit all the right notes, and as is always the case with box-office successes, it paved the way for a flood of films in the gross-out genre. But something was different. Unlike previous films in the genre, there was something more to *Anchorman* and its successors: something deeper but also gentler than what films like *There's Something about Mary* had produced. Whatever this thing was, it worked; as of this writing, in the summer of 2011, with the success of *Bridesmaids* featuring *SNL* alumni Kristin Wiig and Maya Rudolph, the gross-out comedy is still alive and well.

Apatow's films have been criticized for their sentimentality, but those critics confuse authentic human interactions and response for sentimentality, at least in the dismissive sense with which they are using the term. The sentimentality they apply to Apatow's films is a contrived, transparent manipulation of the audience, usually found in made-for-television movies. This type of story relies solely on a melodramatic plot device, such as a terminal illness, to drive its story and its characters clichéd responses. These stories have a fundamental lack of sophistication and intelligence, unlike the work of Apatow and his colleagues.

Apatow's films flesh out comedic archetypes and allow them moments of unflinching honesty. Regardless of the circumstances, the characters are always given full integrity by the actors and writers creating them. The constant in all these films is the strong moral compass of the protagonists, who at the end of the day always take the moral high road.

There are few better examples of the tenet of "entering through their door" than Apatow's films. In the midst of all the grotesque antics, the films have an unwavering message of moral responsibility and compassion for those around us. The titular character in *The 40-Year-Old Virgin* is a perfect example of Apatow's unwavering ethical backbone: the character seemingly held up for derision by the title and early interactions with other characters ultimately proves to be the hero by staying true to his convictions, not only abstaining from premarital sex but also by becoming a present and invested father figure for his girlfriend's children.

Apatow continually goes against the grain of contemporary expectations while also recognizing the importance of entertaining his audience. The films of Apatow gracefully balance that tension between art and evangelization by providing a nonthreatening milieu for the films' target audience (men between the ages of eighteen and thirty-four) that, because of the quality and transcendent message of the content, appeals to all demographics.

*

I'm on the verge. Of what, I'm not exactly sure. As I write this, I am finishing my regency at Loyola Academy after three years of growth, joy, and deepening faith. In the coming months I will begin my theology studies, beginning my final stretch of formation that will eventually lead to the finish line, also known as ordination.

Later this year (2012) I will be bringing a one-man show to the Edinburgh Fringe Festival, as writing and performing once more takes its rightful place in my life.

I began writing this book in large part to discover how and if it were possible to reconcile faith and humor. Two years and many cans of diet soda later, I can say that I've learned they were never apart: humor and faith are an eternal coalescence. Humor, acting as the keystone for the faith that carried me through the death of my father, an angry childhood, and the complications of young adulthood; together they have brought me safely landed to where I am today.

And so now, I honor my sense of humor as a gift from God, no longer a means to a professional or personal end, but a Grace in its own right, a particular way of observing my life and the world around me which makes things better; which makes me better. There is something quite extraordinary about the humor we find in the midst of our ordinary lives, that each moment of laughter we share with a spouse, child, parent, friend, colleague or stranger on the street is in fact a moment in the presence of the Divine. And so it would seem that when it comes to encountering God, sometimes sitting in front of the television works just as well as an altar.

About the Author

Jake Martin, SJ, is a Jesuit comedian and writer from Chicago. He is a regular contributor to *America* magazine and *Busted Halo* and performs stand-up and improvisational comedy in Chicago and New York. Jake is currently studying at the Jesuit School of Theology in Berkeley, California.